FRUITFUL LIVING

FRUITFUL LIVING

A STUDY OF THE FRUIT OF THE SPIRIT FROM GALATIANS 5

BY REV. RONALD W. MIXER

ISBN - 979-8656148153

DEDICATIONS
ACKNOWLEDMENTS

I want to dedicate this work to the following and acknowledge the invaluable help each of the following provided; often unknown to them.

To the many people that have contributed to this book without ever knowing; the people of the churches I served in Manchester, Iowa, Richmond and Odessa, Missouri, and Triumphant Life Church in Lonsdale and Faribault, Minnesota.

To two of my best friends, Martin Perryman and John Otto, I say thank you. Martin because you showed me we still could do it in retirement and John for all the prayer and encouragement over these past 40 years.

Thank you, Glenda, Rachelle and Danielle, my wife and daughters. You took the brunt of my struggles to come to grips with each of these fruits. I know at times it was not easy as I struggled with patience and self-control. Yet we persevered together and I am better for it.

A special thank you to Glenda for her immense help with the editing and cover.

PROLOGUE

I have retitled this book several times, each time I do I think I need to rethink the title. There was a time it was titled Basic Training, but I felt the title was too militaristic. As I ministered within a parachurch organization serving both the Protestant and Catholic world in the 1990's, I served with some in that community that thought even "Onward Christian Soldiers" needed to be forgotten because it was too military; and the "Salvation Army" should be renamed the Salvation Group.

Anything that had to do with a military mindset had to go because we were, as Christians, to be all about love. Then I got back into the real world, and became a pastor again. I began to see the battles people faced every day. They were the same ones they faced when I started this project, and they are the same one's people face as I am ending this project some 30 years after starting.

Yeah, it has taken me over 30 years to write this. I made a huge mistake in the beginning that I am only now able to admit. I did not trust what God had given me as a revelation of Himself to be trustworthy. I have languished in the mire of not feeling old enough, experienced enough, educated enough, and important enough to put these words to press.

Now I realize my mistake, I was not trusting enough of my God and Father to let the world see what I saw in the Scripture those many years ago. I have asked for forgiveness and now you have my thoughts to read. In the words of Paul, the Apostle, to Timothy:

> *Prescribe and teach these things. Let no one look down on your youthfulness, but rather in speech,*

conduct, love, faith and purity, show yourself an example of those who believe. Until I come, give attention to the public reading of Scripture, to exhortation and teaching.

1 Timothy 4:11-13 NASB

So here is what I perceive to be the basics of developing a Fruitful Christian Life. Provided herein are tools to win the battles of the Christian life. They are simple to grasp, hard to develop, and they are easily lost. You must work at producing these fruits daily. When you work at it, practice them and allow the Holy Spirit to develop them within you, you will find strength for the battle.

Ron Mixer

INTRODUCTION

The purpose of this study is to develop within the individual the opportunity for growth that will be in keeping with the teachings of Christ and the whole of the revealed word of God. For years I called it Basic Training. It is more than that, it is blueprint for Fruitful Living.

Without the basics we can flounder in our walk with Christ. During my years as a pastor and para-church minister I was asked many times "how can I be a better Christian?" Talk about a loaded question. Too often we offer simplistic comments as pray more, read your Bible more, get to church more, give more. None of which get to the core of how we should live. We need real life help on the basics. Herein you will find a discussion on the "Fruit of the Spirt." These nine "fruits" are the basis of living a Godly life, and seeking to master each of the nine will accomplish being a better Christian.

Jesus in speaking to His disciples in John 15 states:

> "I am the true vine, and My Father is the vinedresser. "Every branch in Me that does not bear fruit, He takes away; and every branch that bears fruit, He prunes it so that it may bear more fruit. "You are already clean because of the word which I have spoken to you. "Abide in Me, and I in you. As the branch cannot bear fruit of itself unless it abides in the vine, so neither can you unless you abide in Me. "I am the vine, you are the branches; he who abides in Me and I in him, he bears much fruit, for apart from Me you can do nothing. "If anyone does not abide in Me, he is thrown away as a branch and dries up; and they gather them, and cast them into the fire and they are burned. "If you abide in Me,

and My words abide in you, ask whatever you wish, and it will be done for you. "My Father is glorified by this, that you bear much fruit, and so prove to be My disciples. John 15:1-8 NASB

One of the most basic challenges of the Christian life is contained in this passage. Bear fruit. More often than not we think in terms of bringing people to a saving knowledge of Jesus Christ when we read this passage. I want to challenge you to read this passage in light of Galatians 5:22, 23; the named Fruit of the Spirit. It is this fruit that will attract others to Christ, and the lack of this fruit will cause them to reject Christ,

Within the pages of this book you will find the attack methods of the enemy of your soul. The very things that cause you to falter and fail in these nine areas. Along with the attack information, you will find tools for combating the attacks.

If you truly want to be a "better Christian" this book may just be for you. If you are "young in Christ" or "old as the hills," I hope you will find a nugget or two that will draw you closer to Christ and enhance your walk with our Savior.

So here is my hat thrown into the ring as it were, as I write about what I consider the nine most important parts of the Christian walk found in Galatians 5:22, 23.

Rev. Ronald W. Mixer
Piedmont, OK

TABLE OF CONTENTS

Acknowledgements vii

Prologue viii

Introduction x

Table of Contents...xiii

Chapter One: LAYING OUT THE BASICS 1

Chapter Two: THE FRUIT OF LOVE 11

Chapter Three: THE FRUIT OF JOY................................ 23

Chapter Four: THE FRUIT OF PEACE 53

Chapter Five: THE FRUIT OF Patience 72

Chapter Six: THE FRUIT OF KINDNESS 91

Chapter Seven: THE FRUIT OF GOODNESS 109

Chapter Eight: THE FRUIT OF FAITH(FULLNESS) 122

Chapter Nine: THE FRUIT OF MEEKNESS 139

Chapter Ten: THE FRUIT OF TEMPERANCE 153

Chapter Eleven: TOOLS FOR SHARING...........................166

ADDENDUM A: THIRTY DAY READING GUIDE...........186

ADDENDUM B: SEEKING GOD................................. 187

BIBLIOGRAPHY: 189

CHAPTER ONE

LAYING OUT THE BASICS

But the fruit of the Spirit is love, joy, peace, patience, kindness, goodness, faithfulness, gentleness, self-control; against such things there is no law.

Galatians 5:22-23 NASB

As you read this book you will look at the fruits to discover the attributes that Christians want to develop in our lives to bring about a more Christ like life. You will discover from the Scriptures the following three basic ideas concerning the Fruit of the Spirit. You shall explore the fruit as:

1. An attribute of God.

2. As an emotional response of man and the intimate relationship of agape and philao love to the full development of these fruits.

3. The antithesis of each of the fruit and man's attempted regulation, and the influence of satan (I never capitalize the name of the oppressor of the Christian, it is personal, but I choose not to give him any worth) on the nature of man in the struggles to live the fruit of the Spirit.

Understanding is one thing, application is yet another. A combatant that knows the weapon of his warfare, but has never fired the weapon is of little use in battle. It is the same with the fruit of the Spirit. You can know all about the fruit, but if it is not active in your life, you do not have the fruit. Therefore, in each chapter there is a fourth element:

4. With each chapter on the Fruit you will find a collection of Scripture to help with development of the designated fruit.

As a part of this study we will consider the text of I Corinthians 13, Galatians 5:19-26 and Matthew 5:1-12. We shall also attempt to establish practical guidelines for developing each of the fruit in the life of the believer. If we fail in these goals let us all realize that when speaking of the fruit of the Spirit we are subject to our personal understandings of what each of the fruit truly represents. Enduring patience for me may be but a simple trifle of inconvenience for you, and may be yet an exceptional display of control for another.

It is interesting to note, as we begin this study, that two things are very much a part of the subject of fruit. First, it is often said that the apple was the fruit of choice for deceiving Eve and then Adam and causing the fall from grace in the Garden of Eden. Secondly, that in the process of attempting to grow fruit, that it is impossible to do so without the aid of a second plant for effective pollination the fruit tree that you are hoping will bear fruit.

I suggest to you that the fruit of the Spirit will not develop in your life without the aid of another to spur you on in the development and growth in your life. I also submit to you that such growth will involve the act of the Master Gardener to do the much-needed pruning that He does and continues to do in each of our lives. We shall discuss this in light of John 15 at the appropriate time. Having presented these comments and ideas to you the reader, let me encourage you not to drop your pursuit of these Fruit until you have given the Holy Spirit time to completely develop in you the fruit that is so needed in all of us.

As you begin you should read Chapter One and Two as they set the ground work for the rest of the chapters. If patience is more interesting than joy, go ahead and read patience Chapter Five. Then skip to Chapter Ten, if you wish. Chapters Two through Ten will stand alone. Chapter Eleven is about sharing your faith. It should be read only after reading Chapter One. Like any good fruit, savor each chapter and seek to discover how it will change you to develop the Fruit discussed.

THE BEGINNING

We must begin with the thing that is at the beginning of this journey, salvation. We often hear about the wonderful experience of salvation. We boldly proclaim to the convert that they have become new creations and old things have passed away. Often, we give the false and misleading impression that there will now be no more problems in their personal life and that as they have entered the pilgrimage that they will not have to do anything more, having asked for forgiveness and accepting Christ.

We who have been Christians for even a few months know that there is an exceptional amount that we must learn and a tremendous amount of growth that must take place in our lives. Many preachers have had to face the counseling session or visitation opportunity with the new Christian who cannot understand why things are not rosy in every area of their life. With this in mind let me submit to you a diagram and an explanation based upon my understanding of this dilemma.

Referred to as instantaneous and progressive sanctification, this journey is one we all embark upon. The language is theological and not well understood in a practical sense.

non-Christian	Christian
1. Body	1. Spirit
2. Soul mind will emotion	mind will emotion 2. Soul
3. Spirit	3. Body

Diagram 1

As you look at the Diagram 1 note the three-part make-up of man. We most often hear this discussed as the 1. Body, 2. Soul, and 3. spirit. Seldom do we allow the spirit to be relegated to any position other than last. Dead last. Dead and last because in the non-regenerate life there is not a re-birth of the spirit.

Outside of salvation the spirit of man that communes with God, is dead. Paul writing in Romans declares that:

> *"But sin, taking opportunity through the commandment, produced in me coveting of every kind; for apart from the Law sin is dead. I was once alive apart from the Law; but when the commandment came, sin became alive and I died; and this commandment, which was to result in life, proved to result in death for me; for sin, taking an opportunity through the commandment, deceived me and through it killed me."* Romans 7:8-11 NASB

The current rise in the pornographic selling in America and the world is a simple, but graphic, example of the carnal mind set as we explore the first area of the non-Christian or carnal human being. The average American child or adult cannot turn on the television, look to the magazines or newspapers of today without having his or her senses assaulted with advertising promoting sensual responses. It is no longer necessary to purchase pornographic materials to feed the lust of America, one must only turn on the TV to watch the news and he or she will be assaulted by the commercials. We do not need to discuss this further as it is not the theme of this document but merely sited for example.

The second area of the human condition we shall see is the soul. Often this area of man is described as the mind, will, and emotions of man. This definition will fit our purposes satisfactorily. The second area of this assault is the mind. The over-ridding theme of our day is that education is the answer to everything. I will never say that education is not important

> *Study to show thyself approved unto God, a workman that needs not to be ashamed, rightly dividing the word of truth.* 2 Timothy 2:15 KJV[1]

Education alone will not fix the ills of our society. The examples of this are so many that it would be unfair to name any names but consider the insider trading on wall street among the wiz-kids, the down fall of a President, the down fall of the speaker of the house, and many other numerous and varied examples.

The area of the will is another area that is filled with examples of problems, Hitler is but one example of many within the 20th century of those who imposed their will at the cost of human life and the destruction of society. It continues today in the 21st century as celebrities and others seek to demand that everyone think as they think about a myriad of political issues.

We need to look no further than the rising number of psychologists and psychiatrists in our world to realize we have some major emotional problems. One in six or 13% of Americans are on antidepressants as of 2013, the latest year for which I was able to find results. As I visited with a pastor recently he said 85% of the people he counsels are depressed or on anti-depressants.

I am not bashing a serious discipline, psychology and psychiatry, but we must recognize that these are problems in our world and that they are part of the manipulation of the non-Christian and Christian society. Much of what we are fed through the media tells us that we can experience good emotions from the pursuit of things. When this fails to materialize in the individuals' life the door is open for additional psycho-trauma. In some it may manifest as a letdown, in others sadness, in some depression.

The third area of life, that of the spirit, is often left to take care of itself, and it died when the commandment came. We are taught by subtle means that spiritual stuff is for the old, the very young and the not too glamorous, and that among men it is the real nerds, the book worms that seek out God. Years ago, the women's movement declared since church is often a male domain; church and Christianity are tools for the oppression of women.

On the right-hand side of Diagram 1 you will see the Christian side of our diagram. Immediately we notice that the roles of the individual have reversed itself. The spirit now comes first. In salvation the old dead man of Romans 7 is made alive to the newness of life in Christ Jesus and spiritual things become of extreme importance. Paul in

Romans 8 admonishes us to walk after the Spirit and to be led by the Spirit of God, yet he teaches us in I Corinthians 2:11 that to know the things of the Spirit of God they must be learned by the spirit of man. For us to be led and learn we must first be alive. Salvation allows for this wonderful experience of knowing God on a personal basis and the opportunity to follow the things of God.

Next let us examine the third element of the Christian side of our diagram. We will return to the second further on in our discussion.

Paul writes several times about the body, and the need to keep the body under subjection. For this reason, we have placed the dividing line above the body. We as Christians are to crucify the flesh and deny the lustful desires of the flesh. If we are successful in bringing the body under control this will allow us more freedom to develop the area of the spiritual man and the soul with Christ like fruit. Let us examine carefully the Scripture and apply them to our personal life. We should note that as we continue we will discuss this concept in greater detail when we discuss the area of temperance in relation to the fruit.

Turning our attention to the second area of the Christians life, the soul we discover one of the most perplexing problems the new Christian must face. That is part of his/her life that keeps returning from those experiences prior to salvation. We often associate this experience with temptation. Let us go back to the diagram once more and observe that the mind, will and emotions have not changed in the order of importance and have not changed in that we do not forget everything we have learned. If we have learned to cry at certain stimulus we will still cry at the same time. If we learn to use vulgar language before salvation then we still know the words, their meaning, and how to use them.

Temptation encourages us to use them, thus opening the door for guilt and the destruction of the relationship started at salvation. It is my observation that there is just one area of the soul that does undergo a significant change at salvation, and that is the will. I believe that it is because for salvation to be complete it requires a commitment of self and a willingness to serve God for people to be saved.

Without a willingness to serve God, the salvation message falls upon the ears of the self-seeking who are looking for a better existence. This is played out repeatedly in the rescue missions of this world, when the client comes in and professes salvation to get a meal to satisfy the flesh. This is not to diminish the mission work or workers, for many lives are changed by the selfless work and ministry of those who serve the Lord in this area of Christian endeavor, but simply stated for example.

If we are to become what Christ taught us to be, then some radical things must happen in our lives. I believe that the sanctification (the act of cleansing the soul from sin), that is the instantaneous sanctification, takes place in the spirit of man, whereas the progressive changing sanctification takes place in the soul, in the mind, the will and the emotions. Paul writes in Ephesians:

> *"That he might sanctify and cleanse it* (the church of which we are members of) *with the washing of the water by the word."*   Ephesians 5:26 KJV
>   (Parentheses' mine)

Consider also Ephesians:

and that you be renewed in the spirit of your mind
Ephesians 4:23 NASB

It is by using our mind that we are can absorb the cleansing word of God. We are then able to be cleansed and purified in the mind and the soul. It must be understood that in the act of salvation the Spirit of God brings the spirit of man alive again and that old things do pass away and we are clean. We, however, have the task before us of keeping clean and of keeping the relationship alive. We do that by the study of God's Word, the Bible, the hearing of God's Word, the sermons on Sunday, the engrafting of God's Word, the meditation and thinking on the ways of God. In doing so we hide the word in our hearts that we might not sin against God (See Psalm 119:11).

Before I can allow you the reader to continue I must ask have you personally received Jesus Christ as Lord and Savior in your life? If you are uncertain then let me encourage you to do so right now. If you have any reservations or need questions answered I encourage you to seek out a Pastor or someone you know is a Christian and ask them to lead you into a saving relationship with Jesus before you read any further in this book. If you know you need Christ and there are no questions other than whether you are a Child of God through salvation here is a simple prayer to pray:

"Jesus, I come to you now as a person in need of salvation. I acknowledge I have sinned and I fall short of what You have called me to be as Your child. I repent of my sins and ask for Your cleansing blood to wash away the sins of my life. Please set me on the path to live my life for You.

Teach me Your ways that I might be Your child from this day forward. Amen."

If you have prayed this simple prayer, you can rest assured that your sins are washed away. You are a new creature in Christ Jesus. There is much to learn as a Christian and you need other Christians to help you grow. Find a Bible believing church near you that you can become a part of and seek out people that can help you grow. This book starts with some of the basics, so hang on. Here we go.

We are now ready to consider the fruit of the Spirit. In the fruit we shall see how they are closely tied to our emotions and emotional responses and their relationship to the development of the Christians life. We will see how the enemy uses the raw emotions to cause us to stumble. How the numbing of emotion defeats the fruit in us from growing. We shall also discover the beauty of God as we look at each fruit as part of whom the revealed God is to us and how He shines through in each fruit.

CHAPTER TWO

THE FRUIT OF LOVE

"Beloved let us love one another for love is of God and everyone that loves is born of God and knows God, He that loves not knows not God, for <u>God is LOVE</u>."

I John 4:7, 8 NASB

Books have been written about it, movies have been filmed, and Children's stories have been compiled, all in a futile effort to define and to promote "TRUE LOVE".

"True Love" in the previous paragraph, is the added ingredient that saves the hero or heroine from the foe as they are locked in mortal combat with some unyielding and dangerous fiend. It is true love that gives them the strength to overcome the seemingly impossible odds that are stacked against them.

The statement that "true love" will protect us from the evil onslaught of the fictional kind is buried within the tremendous truth of the agape love of God and His son Jesus Christ. "True Love" of the spiritual kind will protect us, and deliver us, from the onslaught of the enemy of our souls, the "True Love" of God.

We turn our attention to the first fruit, love, and begin to examine it as an attribute of God.

LOVE AS AN ATTRIBUTE

Webster's New College Dictionary[1] defines attribute as "an inherent characteristic, an object closely associated with or belonging to a specific person, thing, or office."

When we look at who God is, we will see those closely associated characteristics, His attributes. Perhaps John said it best when he wrote:

> *Beloved, let us love one another, for love is from God; and everyone who loves is born of God and knows God. The one who does not love does not know God, for God is love.*   *1 John 4:7-8 NASB*

When everything that can be written is written on the subject of love, one fact will remain, that is simply this: God is LOVE. His sacrificial gift of His only begotten Son, Jesus Christ, is to us an example of the depth and intensity of His love. His example is one that He does not expect us to imitate or emulate. The best we could hope to do is found in the text of the book of Romans:

> *For while we were still helpless (sinners in KJV), at the right time Christ died for the ungodly.* ***For one will hardly die for a righteous man; though perhaps for the good man someone would dare even to die.*** *But God demonstrates His own love toward us, in that while we were yet sinners, Christ died for us.*   Romans 5:6-8 NASB
> (bold text mine)

We see this great God, the God of the entire universe involved, actively involved, in the lives of His people throughout both the Old and New Testaments. Let us look at just two examples.

Our first example is Jerimiah. God speaks to Jeremiah about His love for him.

> *"The LORD appeared to him from afar, saying, "I have loved you with an everlasting love; Therefore I have drawn you with lovingkindness."*
>
> Jeremiah 31:3 NASB

If we personalize this passage for Jerimiah, it would look like below. Don't hesitate to insert your own name.

The LORD appeared to <u>Jeremiah</u> from afar, saying, "I have loved you, <u>Jeremiah,</u> with an everlasting love; Therefore, I have drawn you, <u>Jeremiah,</u> with lovingkindness.

Within the society of today, we often hear of people falling out of love, and divorce destroying the family unit. God gives us the example here of the depth and persistence of His love, "I have loved you with an everlasting love," He declares. Not until God gets mad at us, not until we let Him down, not until we fail in some disastrous way. But, with an everlasting, unending love a love that knows no limitations or inability. You cannot get God to stop loving you. You can try, but you will fail. He does not know the word quit when it comes to loving you

Our second example is found in the Gospel of John:

> *"This is My commandment, that you love one another, just as I have loved you. "Greater love has no one than this, that one lay down his life for his friends. "You are My friends if you do what I command you.*   John 15:12-14 NASB

We must note here that this verse gives us two examples of this magnificent love that God has for us, first, Jesus was here, on the face of the earth interacting with the men we call His disciples. God did not have to send His Son, but He did. Second, Jesus gives a foreshadowing here of the love that would take Him to the cross, and keep Him hanging there until death won that initial and only victory.

Paul the Apostle writing to the Romans gave us the assurance that God will still be involved in our lives even at this late hour in history.

And we know that God causes all things to work together for good to those who love God, to those who are called according to His purpose.
Romans 8:28 NASB

We must realize that this involvement is conditional upon our involvement with Him. We find, in the continuation of this passage, in verse 35 and verses 38 and 39 that Paul lists 17 specific and general (see table 1) categories of influence that will not be able to separate us from the love of God and the love of Christ.

THINGS THAT CANNOT SEPARATE US – ROMANS 8:35,38,39		
TRIBULATION	SWORD	THINGS TO COME
DISTRESS	DEATH	POWERS
PERSECUTION	LIFE	HEIGHT
FAMINE	ANGELS	DEPTH
NAKEDNESS	PRINCIPALITIES	OTHER CREATIONS
PERIL	THINGS PRESENT	

TABLE 1

The only possible exception available here is the individual. We control our own personal destiny in experiencing the love of God at work in our own life. God's involvement with us depends upon our personal involvement with Him.

LOVE AS AN EMOTION

Let us now turn our attention to the second area of concern, the fruit as an emotional response in Man.

I believe it is not possible to effectively develop the capacity for love and to love without the involvement of another. Love does not happen in a vacuum. God could not love the "World" until He created the "World." It was in the heart and mind of God from the foundations of the world to love His creation, and to give Himself for that creation in the ultimate act of and expression of Love (See Ephesians 1:4; 1Peter 1:20; Matthew 25:34; Luke 11:50; Hebrews 4:3; Hebrews 9:26; Revelation 13:8; Revelation 17:8)

We see the benevolent, loving God of the universe, with everything that could satisfy at His whim and command, soundly in control of the universe, creating man. I must tell you that if it was me in charge I am not sure that I would have created us.

God creates us so:
1. He might have a companion to walk with in the cool of the day, (Genesis 3:8-9)
2. That there might be people upon whom He might demonstrate the depth of His Love. Revelation 13:8 (NASB) gives us just a glimpse of the fact that this was God's plan that Christ would die for us. *"All who dwell on the earth will worship him, everyone whose name has not been written from the foundation of the world in the book of life of the Lamb who has been slain. "*
3. That He might inhabit our Praise and Worship. (See Psalm 22:3; Jeremiah 33:11; Hebrew 13:15; 1Peter 2:9)

For all that God is, and all that He possesses, none of His love would have been known, except He created humanity, with whom He might have interaction and the opportunity to express His love. Void of human contact we would (and do) become reclusive and hermit like, unloving and un-caring.

Of the four basic human emotions the love/hate emotion elicits the greatest amount of response. We often miss interpret the sensual stimulus of the flesh as the love/hate emotion, particularly among the young. The more mature person should know the difference between sexual impulse and love in its purer and more mature form. But, love is often turned to hatred, by the indiscretion of not differentiating between the two.

Hence, the spouse who discovers a cheating mate, the businessman who discovers an embezzling employee, or equal that is cheating the company, and the possibilities are endless, provides the stage for severe changes in the emotional response.

That we can hate so easily is indeed frightening, but alas, love and hate are very intimate, and we must choose how we will respond. The mature Christian will always choose, even when he/she does not want too, to love. It is this basic human emotion that separates the Christian from the non-Christian. John records the words of Jesus on this subject

> "A new commandment I give to you, that you love one another, even as I have loved you, that you also love one another. "By this all men will know that you are My disciples, if you have love for one another."
> John 13:34-35 NASB

It is by this simple act of choosing love over hate that we are able to demonstrate to the entire world, Jesus.

Mike Warnke[2], a Christian comedian of the 1970's and 1980's tells of how in navy boot camp two young men who were Christians demonstrated this love to him in every facet of life, even when Warnke punched one in the face and broke his nose, they would not stop telling him the message of God's love. It was the foremost item on these young men's agenda, to share the message of God's love with Warnke.

It was because of this genuine love in the midst of navy boot camp that Warnke became a Christian. The young man easily could have punched back and who of us would have blamed him, but instead with blood running down his face, Warnke relates, he again told of the warmth of God's love. Warnke was broken by the love of God, and in that moment, a hardened heart melted.

To love, in the difficult situations, may indeed be the hardest challenge of the Christian walk, but it is the commandment of Christ. It is not a suggestion for consideration; it is an obligation, a duty, a commandment. When we consider the close link between love and hate we begin to see with clarity the importance of the love factor.

LOVE'S ANTITHESIS

Let us now turn our attention to the other side of the coin, the antithesis of the love of God. I remember a few years ago hearing a radio broadcast, and I believe David Mains[3] was the speaker, and he suggested, even implied with great import, that the true opposite of love was not hate, but apathy. Even though hate is the dark side of love, apathy is the absence of love, or even for that matter, the absence of hate.

I have used this information many times and nearly every time I suggest apathy as the opposite of love, there is a firestorm of disagreement. My conclusion concerning this is that we want anger/hate/malice to be the opposite. I came to this conclusion because apathy as an opposite shows us our failing in reaching the world with the love of God. It is easy to say I do not hate, have anger or malice. It is next to impossible to say I do not have apathy. We use our apathy to excuse ourselves from witnessing, funding, and promoting the gospel with a simple "I did not feel led to do such and such."

Apathy is a nothing in the emotional sense. The isolated person will not hate, nor shall he/she love. The apathetic person will have simply no use for anyone else, and the intensity of their apathy will continue to grow as the years pass unless there is a sudden stimulus for change. That stimulus will either awaken the hatred/love emotion or they will dive deeper into apathy. Hatred and love will both set the soul on fire and consume the mind, will and emotions, but apathy quenches all such flames.

When we consider the role of satan in the fruit of love we must realize his goal is apathy. We must not overlook the fact that he is the author of apathy. Jesus in speaking to the church at Philadelphia in Revelation notes:

> *I know your deeds, that you are neither cold nor hot; I wish that you were cold or hot. 'So, because you are lukewarm, and neither hot nor cold, I will spit you out of My mouth.*   Revelation 3:15-16 NASB

A clearer picture of apathy could not be written. Applied here to the spiritual we can easily see the application to the love/hate/apathy discussion.

Amos put the best of the love hate emotion into action when he wrote "Hate evil, love good, and establish justice in the gate! ... Amos 5:15 NASB

Recognize the vital link between the way you feel about something and the way you could feel when love and hate are concerned, and then choose whether you will be known for your love or if you will be just another person walking the face of the earth, toying with the idea of apathy.

LOVE IN ACTION

If you are married and you find that you are disconnected to your spouse and it seems you no longer know how to "love" your spouse let me recommend a simple book that has stood the test of time as a reading assignment. _The Five Love Languages_, by Dr. Gary Chapman[4]. There are several editions of this wonderful easy to read and understand book. I confess I read it every time I meet with a couple seeking counseling for their marriage or wanting to get married. If you will make the applications of the book you will find it easier to love the spouse God has given you.

Okay, you are not married, or your marriage is good and yet you know you need to up your game in the area of loving people. Here are a few suggestions:
> 1. Teach a child about love by helping someone who is in need. Volunteer at a mission in your area, and not just at the holidays. Better yet,

start with yourself. Find a place you can give out of love to those in need; you cannot teach what is not real to yourself. If you do not have compassion and love for someone in need, you cannot teach it to others.

2. Sit at the mall, or any place where there are multitudes of people passing near you. Look at each one and remind yourself they are headed to a Godless hell if someone does not tell them of the Grace and Love of God. Stay there until your heart is broken for the lost in front of you.

3. Search for a reason to talk to someone about the Love that Christ has shown in your life. Then go do it.

4. Consider the one person you dislike the most. Spend one minute a day for the next week praying a blessing on their life. Keep a journal of what you pray. At the end of the week evaluate your feelings toward the person and read the book of Jonah. Are you a Jonah? Do you sit under the tree and sulk because God is blessing the one you do not want blessed? Or, has God melted your heart? Pray for a melting.

5. Using a good concordance, electronic Bible[5] or any Bible resource that you have available to look for as many passages on Love in the Bible you can find. Meditate on how you can incorporate the love expressed in the passages into your own life.

6. Choose an action of Love for this day and be consistent with everyone you encounter, family friends, co-workers and strangers and seek to give them your chosen expression of love for that day. Do not make it complicated, a simple comment on how much they mean to you or impact you, can be all that is needed to start the process in your life.

The fastest way to develop love is to discover the Love of Christ for a lost world. Unless you are connected to the world around you by some act, you are operating in apathy. You must connect to people to begin to be able to express the Love of Christ. If you have received Christ into your life, you are the recipient of that love. You will need to cultivate it so you too can love. Jesus admonishes with this:

> *A new commandment I give to you, that you love one another, even as I have loved you, that you also love one another.* John 13:34 NASB

When love seems to be elusive, and you are struggling to love someone in any given situation, it is appropriate to:
1. Stop; remember the Love God had for you that caused Him to send His Son for your salvation.
2. Mentally review where you would be without His love.
3. Consider the person you are struggling with in light of yourself. Nevertheless, except for the grace of God that person is you.

It is extremely important that we as Christians never stop trying to grow in the grace that comes from the Love of God in our lives. When we stop loving we are in danger of developing apathy, and the enemy wins. The Bible tells us that:

> *But in all these things we overwhelmingly conquer through Him who loved us.* Romans 8:37 NASB

I concede that it can be said that I took this verse out of the context in which it is written. Making that concession I also want to point out that the list that follows in verses 38 and 39 has one glaring omission. What omission you may ask? Look for yourself in the list. There is nothing, in heaven or earth that can keep you from the Love of God. Except you. When we stop pursuing God, apathy sets in, the enemy wins and the only thing missing from the list loses.

To love is a constant effort. It is the basis for all the fruit as we shall see in coming chapters, and we can never be fully formed and have the Fruit of the Spirit without it.

CHAPTER THREE

THE FRUIT OF JOY

*And the disciples were continually filled with joy
and with the Holy Spirit.*   Acts 13:52 NASB

...for the joy of the LORD is your strength.
                    Nehemiah 8:10 NASB

Joy! For thousands of years man has pursued the illusive quality of joy. Money, we are told, cannot buy happiness. Some would say that it could buy a moment of respite from the ordinary, yet even that is but for a fleeting moment of time and fades very quickly.

Yet, the airwaves of our world in the twenty first century are jammed with the message that to have joy we must purchase this, that, or another thing. We even have a dish detergent that has the distinct honor of being designated "JOY," as if the sheer purchase and use of this particular product will bring us to a level of ecstasy. Such ecstasy will then result in the wellbeing and euphoria that we associate with, and joy will be present.

Keeping in mind, we talk about and yet see very little representation of this quality of life, joy. Let us begin to pursue the fruit of the Spirit in the area of the Fruit of Joy. Look with me at Webster's definition of joy.

> The emotion evoked by well-being, success, or good fortune or by the prospect of possessing what one desires: Delight; the expression or exhibition of such emotion; Gaiety a state of happiness or felicity; Bliss a source or cause of delight (v). to experience great pleasure or delight, rejoice.

We must ask at this point if this definition does justice to the concept of Biblical joy. It would seem that a few important details are missing, such as, the emotion of well-being that is evoked by the knowledge of God's constant and abiding love for us. The emotion that pushes to the very surface of our skin when we see a new babe in Christ moments after the initial profession of faith and confession of Jesus Christ as Lord and Savior.

It also seems important to this writer to address the much-used cliché that joy equals J=Jesus, O=Others y=you (note small y on you). Is this truly joy? Some will strongly disagree with my personal stand and defend the integrity of the cliché as being totally accurate, and for that person I would suggest that they will find themselves among the givers and caregivers of the motivational gifts of Romans 12.

However, for many within the body of Christ their personal joy is being destroyed trying to live up to the demands of Jesus, Others, you. At best this should be held as a goal but not a command.

The individuals that become intent upon these clichés are most often motivated by the needs of others, and often get the perspective of Jesus first out of synch in their pursuit of the needs of a few. There must be a realization that for Jesus to be first the individual must take time for himself.

Time for study of the word, time for spiritual refreshing, time for prayer, and time for his/her family relationships lest there becomes a feeling within the person of resentment for the time and effort spent on others.

As with any axiom for living, this cliché must be taken in the balance of all of God's word. It would indeed be tragic to save the lives of many and meet the needs of many, only to discover the loss of family, personal health, or personal faith.

As ministers we hear much about pastoral burnout, and indeed I have been there, therefore let me suggest a new term for pastoral burn out, career suicide. Indeed, this term may be applied to other areas of employment but I feel this most effectively describes what I see happening to Pastors. Often the load of trying to put others first, and not taking time for personal interests causes such feelings of resentment that career suicide opens the door for escape. Escape from Jesus, Others and nothing; nothing because all is given in the pursuit of living up to the demands of J.O.y.

Having opened this sensitive area to discussion and to obvious feelings of frustration how then shall we reconcile this area of Joy with the proposed concept that true anything, in the Fruit of the Spirit, cannot develop without love as a beginning point. Let us back track to the previous chapter and remind ourselves that God is Love and that He loves us with an everlasting love.

We also need to remember as we begin our study that the only realm of our society that offers an opportunity for real Joy is in the realm of the church. We hear less and less about joy and more and more about happiness, self-fulfillment, and getting what we want. We need to realize that joy comes from contentment in whatever our situation.

> Not that I speak from want, for I have learned to be content in whatever circumstances I am.
> Philippians 4:11 NASB

With this in mind and in pursuit of establishing a Biblical basis for joy and developing true joy in our lives, let us examine several Scriptures to discover if indeed God, who is love is also the God of Joy.

JOY AS AN ATTRIBUTE

It would indeed be wonderful to open the Bible to a verse that said God is Joy, but alas, there is none. Nor will there be in the continuation of this study a specific verse that will show us the attribute we wish to see whether it be joy or meekness. We shall not have the advantage of a single descriptive verse as we had in the first fruit, however we will find adequate Scripture portions to demonstrate the fruit as it relates to God.

We begin with Genesis 1:10,12,18,21,25, and 31. Each of the preceding verses has one phrase in common, "and God saw that it was good." Verse 31 goes one step further and God declares creation to be very good. Just this simple added declarative "very" gives us insight into the pleasure God was taking from His handiwork. It was a feeling perhaps of a successful completion of the task at hand.

Return briefly with me to the definition of joy and we find joy as the emotion that is evoked by success. God had succeeded in His creation, and we can anticipate that there was joy at that moment. If we had to stop here for our insight we of course would be on very shaky turf, but we don't.

Let us press on to Nehemiah 8:10 and we find Nehemiah sending the people to feast with a notation to care for the less fortunate, and the declaration that "the joy of the Lord is their strength." As we ponder this passage it is important to see that we benefit from the joy of the Lord as it becomes our strength, it is both His and ours. It is His joy, in us that produces the strength.

When we look at this verse we must see that it is God's joy made real and rich in us that gives us the feeling of contentment that allows us to be strong in the most difficult time. Again, I sense we have had to reach a little to see that God has joy from this text, so let us continue to build the case as we examine Job:

> *"Then he will pray to God, and He will accept him, that he may see His face with joy, And He may restore His righteousness to man."* Job 33:26 NASB

Elihu is speaking to Job, and declares it is the Spirit of God that has caused him to speak; and in the preceding verses gives the reasons he held his tongue for so long. Elihu makes this wonderful statement that when Job prays that God will be favorable to him, and he, Job, will see the joy of God's face.

Even if you would read this passage that it is with joy that Job would see God's face we here see established an undeniable link between God's person and joy. Let us press on again this time to Isaiah:

> *"For, behold, I create a new heavens and a new earth: and the former shall not be remembered, nor come into mind. But be glad and rejoice forever in that which I create: for behold, I create Jerusalem a rejoicing, and her people a joy. And I will rejoice in Jerusalem, and joy in my people..."*
> Isaiah 65:17-19 KJV

Here we have the first hard evidence of a God who experiences joy. The dispensationalist will see this as future and place it sometime after the return of Christ.

However, there is sufficient evidence to warrant the placement in the context of historical Israel, and within that setting we see God rejoicing after four centuries with His people, and enjoying the newly established order begun in Isaiah 40. At this juncture it is not necessary to declare one's position on eschatology to identify the fact that we have a God associated with joy.

Let us now consider Zephaniah:

> *"The LORD your God is in your midst, A victorious warrior. He will exult over you with joy, He will be quiet in His love, He will rejoice over you with shouts of joy."*　　　　Zephaniah 3:17 NASB

We need not peruse the Scriptures any further, (but we will), to discover without reservation that God is a God of joy. Joy is a part of His person.

Too often we only see God as the angry tyrant, waiting for us to slip up so He can get us; or as an old grandpa too decrepit or too self-involved to care about us. In these verses, we see a God who takes joy in His creation, rejoices in us, and is involved in our existence. As we look into the New Testament, we discover that all of heaven rejoices when a sinner is saved from eternal damnation by the shed blood of Jesus Christ. (Luke 15:7-10)

God's love keeps Him involved in our lives and He rejoices with us and He has joy because of our existence. It might be presumptuous to express that God delights and finds joy in our discoveries of Him. He has not changed, but we are ignorant of all that He is. As we grow and learn of Him I believe He finds joy in our growth.

Much the same as we find joy in the development of our own children, we find God's pleasure (joy) in the development of His only begotten Son, Jesus. Matthew delineates this for us in his third chapter:

and behold, a voice out of the heavens said, "This is My beloved Son, in whom I am well-pleased."
Matthew 3:17 NASB

The most exciting part of this verse comes when we realize that we are joint-heirs with Jesus Christ, and that Jesus is the first born among many brethren. As God has shown His pleasure with Christ's obedience we can realize that as we are obedient to His Word, we, as His children, will evoke feelings of pleasure and joy for our Heavenly Father.

THE LINK OF LOVE

"But now I come to You; and these things I speak in the world so that they may have My joy made full in themselves. JOHN 17:13 NASB

We now turn our attention to the next vitally important area of this text, the link of Love to our fruit for this section, Joy. It is the commandment of Christ that we should love one another that our joy might be full, so, before we begin to examine the criteria of loving let us first examine Jesus' prayer concerning His joy to be manifest in us.

John declared "...that they might have MY JOY fulfilled in themselves."

Jesus here is praying to the Father just prior to the garden experience that would lead Him to the cross. It is

His prayer that the disciples would know that unity that He and the Father God knew. In knowing that unity they would begin to experience the joy that He, Jesus and the Father, God experience. We turn our attention to the context of this passage in John, where we find the commandment of Christ

> *"If you keep My commandments, you will abide in My love; just as I have kept My Father's commandments and abide in His love. "These things I have spoken to you so that My joy may be in you, and that your joy may be made full. "This is My commandment, that you love one another, just as I have loved you.*
>
> John 15:10-12 NASB

His promise is of fulfilled joy if we comply with and achieve this most honorable degree of love.

The unqualifying, undemanding, totally accepting love for those who are in Christ Jesus that Christ introduces here, is for the body of Christ to practice and establish. We must ask ourselves, how much has the church and body of Christ missed in the area of joy because we have been unwilling, but not unable, to express and demonstrate and proclaim and possess Christ like love?

Joy is one of those child-like feelings that most of us seem to lose as we mature, perhaps it is because we become cynical, fearful, and untrusting and often we simply lack any commitment to love without our qualifying the person we might love. We qualify them on the basis of parents, clothes, appearance, hygiene, cars, home, etc. In so doing we limit the working of God in our life to produce the joy that Christ and the Father possess.

We want joy and we search for it in new Bibles, hoping that some new translation might make it easier to get some new revelation of God. We search so that we might feel closer to Him and obtain joy. We buy clothes because we all know that if we feel confident in what we are wearing we will be happy and have joy.

We get into debt for new cars, and many other baubles. One car manufacturer tells me there is no feeling like owning one of his cars, another that it just feels right, another implies that my heart will not beat right if I do not have theirs. Another brand says that it's winning the world over therefore the implication is that if I want to be a winner I will drive their cars and of course we all know winners are happy and have joy. There are dozens of other baubles and trinkets that are nothing more than objects that we are told we just simply have to own so we can be happy and have joy.

The essence of true joy is found in true love for the body of Christ. If, telling my wife I would marry her all over again necessitates the purchase of a diamond that is bigger than the one I bought her for our engagement, then our relationship is built on things and not love and will fail in the area of joy. If, I purchase such a gift with the correct motivation, then it becomes an expression of my love and not duty.

Joy is content, but it is not complacent. Nehemiah 8:10 gave us one of the glimpses of the joy of the Lord, but it ties itself very closely to action for the oppressed. The Children of Israel were told to make provision for the ones without food or drink, as part of the condition for receiving the joy of the Lord. That joy found in the giving and serving the oppressed would be their strength.

It was necessary for them to exhibit compassion to the less fortunate, it was an expression of their love. We are well aware that if we give that we are blessed for our giving. The Scriptures teach us it is more blessed to give than to receive, (Acts 20:35) and we here have seen the link to joy of being benevolent, yet we will hoard, and provide for our own wants, and wonder why we lack joy.

Jesus said that there was no greater expression of love than this, to lay down one's life for a friend (John 15:13). If that is the greatest depth of love possible, then perhaps we have a glimpse of the commitment to love that is necessary to experience the fullness of joy Jesus spoke and prayed about.

JOY AS EMOTION

The Psalmist wrote:

> *You will make known to me the path of life; In Your presence is fullness of joy; In Your right hand there are pleasures forever.* Psalms 16:11 NASB

If we are in His presence on a continual and regular basis, I believe that we will develop the compassion of God for the world around us and out of that compassion and love will come action and from that action will come joy. Joy that will flood us and compel us to even greater giving of ourselves.

We strive for joy. The evidence is the entertainment industry and the abundance of comedy. Do we mistake laughter for joy? I believe so.

We have somehow developed the illusion that we have joy if we laugh enough. A misconception of my youth was fat people, excuse me, overweight people are jolly, therefore overweight people were happy all the time. In my maturing years I have learned that most overweight people are not happy. More often they are depressed, and out of their depression, eat more than they should, and are often seeking comfort in food rather than relationships. The laughter hides the pain so they laugh.

The problem is laughter is not joy; and if it is not joy, then what is joy?

I have spent much of my life and ministry trying to understand Galatians 5:22-23 the basis of this book. The fruit of the Spirit does not seem complicated on the surface, but there is so much beneath the surface. Let me introduce a few questions regarding these magnificent qualities.

1. How does God and His Spirit figure into these nine fruits?
2. Are there more than nine fruit?
3. Is there any baseline fruit that is needed before the others can be known and exhibited?
4. If these are the fruit is there an opposite for each one?
5. Are there any Scriptural filters for these nine fruits?
6. When should I be concerned about these fruits in my spiritual walk?

I want you to read you something I wrote in the middle of the night when God laid part of this my heart.

FROM JANUARY 2016

The question what is love has eluded me for most of my life. I did not grow up in an overtly loving home. This is not to say I do not love, it is simply to encourage you and to help explore what I have come to believe can be used as a starting point to understand what is joy.

Some of the things love is not: apathy, malicious anger, jealousy, full of bragging, arrogant self-centered, one who retains a grudge, and many more things. Here perhaps the ultimate passage on love. It is read at many weddings and is often used to describe love in the church world.

> *If I speak with the tongues of men and of angels, but do not have love, I have become a noisy gong or a clanging cymbal. If I have the gift of prophecy, and know all mysteries and all knowledge; and if I have all faith, so as to remove mountains, but do not have love, I am nothing. And if I give all my possessions to feed the poor, and if I surrender my body to be burned, but do not have love, it profits me nothing. Love is patient, love is kind and is not jealous; love does not brag and is not arrogant, does not act unbecomingly; it does not seek its own, is not provoked, does not take into account a wrong suffered, does not rejoice in unrighteousness, but rejoices with the truth; bears all things, believes all things, hopes all things, endures all things. Love never fails; but if there are gifts of prophecy, they will be done away; if there are tongues, they will cease; if there is knowledge, it will be done away. For we know in part and we prophesy in part; but when the perfect comes, the partial will be done away. When I was a child, I used to speak like a child, think like a child, reason like a child; when I became a man, I did away with childish things. For now, we see in a mirror dimly, but then face to face; now I know in part, but then I will know fully just*

as I also have been fully known. But now faith, hope, love, abide these three; but the greatest of these is love.

1 Corinthians 13:1-13 NASB

I think I have learned that love is one more thing. I can perhaps explain what I mean before I state the simple words that explain my thought. I have six grandchildren now; it is from them that I am learning the most about love. (I will say the older two (both girls) have me wrapped around their little fingers.) From them I have learned as well. Love is not what I propose but love brings about what I propose. My twin grandsons are perhaps the best at showing me what I am learning, but all six are good at this expression. It is not an expression I experienced with my grandparents as we lived too far away from them to be close. They were foreign to us and the relationships were very stiff.

So, what is this expression that shows love? It is the expression of sheer joy. Love is not joy, nor is every expression of joy, love. But here is what I see and have learned, and am challenged by as I write this in the middle of a cold January night. Do we have a sense of joy when we are with those we say we love? When I surprised my twin grandsons yesterday at daycare picking them up for their mom they got so very happy to see me. (It could be they were just happy to get out of there, but...) All six of the grandchildren call me "Papa." What a thrill it is for me when they yell Papa at the very sight of my face and run to me for a hug and to tell me about their newest toy, or experience, or they went poopy in the toilet (they are toilet training and that is an important event in their lives as I am writing).

There is a joy, and I feel it too. When I think of my other two grandsons it is all about getting tackled and rolling around on the floor with them. They are the youngest and oldest of my grandsons, and wow can they ruff house. We tussle for as long as I can last or until the youngest (who is 2 as of this writing and is going to be the biggest of the boys and is well on his way to being that already) decides to belly flop on me, or jump from a couch with me as the landing zone. During that time the joy flies all around and we know we love and are loved.

With the granddaughters it is the same yet different. It is making pies together (cherry and apple) or lunch at subway or breakfast at IHOP, (I am trying to spoil them so that when they are looking to marry in 20 years they are looking for a husband who will treat them right). There is a joy that comes when we spend the day together, and it begins with a "Papa" and a hug.

Here is my point. There are three times in Scripture that the phrase "Abba Father" is used (they are shown below from the NASB). Romans 8:15, Galatians 4:6, Mark 14:36 Paul said we could call God "Abba Father." That the Spirit of the Son would come into our hearts crying "Abba Father," (note that the ability to call someone "Abba Father" comes only to the direct children of the "Father". This speaks to the adoption into God's family that Christians enjoy). Finally, we see Jesus, the only begotten son, crying out "Abba Father".

> *For you have not received a spirit of slavery leading to fear again, but you have received a spirit of adoption as sons by which we cry out, "Abba! Father!"*   *Romans 8:15 NASB*

> *Because you are sons, God has sent forth the Spirit of His Son into our hearts, crying, "Abba! Father!"*   *Galatians 4:6 NASB*

And He was saying, "Abba! Father! All things are possible for You; remove this cup from Me; yet not what I will, but what You will." Mark 14:36 NASB

It has been said, written, preached, and generally established that the phrase "Abba Father" is akin to saying "Daddy, Daddy."

In our everyday life I would add that the same endearment could also be "Papa, Papa" or "Mimi" (the grandkids name for grandma) or "Mama".

Abba Father is an expression of entitlement. It is an expression of "I am your child!" It can be breathed with pure joy, "Abba...Father," in desperation, "Abba, Father!" But never with disdain or anger or hatred. It can be declared with joy after a long absence "Abba! Father!" or in humility after a failure "Abba, Father". It is generally declared with the essence of love infused within.

When you look at young lovers, you see joy. When you look at grandchildren with their grandparents you should see joy, parents with their children you should see joy.

When my girls were young I traveled during the week most weeks. Their mom did an amazing job being a working mom and single parent during the week. I have two awesome daughters who were found by two awesome men, their husbands. Some of the best memories I have are getting home from a trip and being in the office working and having both girls pile on my lap to tell me about their day at school.

As they got older we broke a couple of chairs (I was 6' 4 1/2" and 250 in those days). We would all squeal when the chairs broke and laugh. There was a lot of joy in those days, not as much as I wish had occurred. In part I was learning how to love and show love. I still am. Joy is not love, but love helps produce joy. Nehemiah states

> *"Then he said to them, "Go, eat of the fat, drink of the sweet, and send portions to him who has nothing prepared; for this day is holy to our Lord.* <u>*Do not be grieved, for the joy of the LORD is your strength.*</u> *"*
>
> Nehemiah 8:10 NASB

Did you notice the last part? I underlined it. The joy of the Lord is your strength. Need a strength boost, get some joy in your life. Don't know how to get joy? Find someone to love, or someone you do love and spend some time with them. Feed someone who is hungry. You will quickly find some joy, and you will grow in love. You just might begin to understand this fruit of the Spirit a bit more. It is a real emotional experience.

JOY'S ANTITHESIS

Let us now turn our attention to the opposite side of the coin, to the down side if you will of joy. Roget's College Thesaurus lists the antonym of joy as dejection and then lists the very first synonym as depression. Our country has experienced what was called the "ME" decade and then "WE" decade. We have seen the large increases in depression and depression related syndromes in recent years[1]. Depression has been blamed as the cause of many social ills and crimes. A husband gets depressed and shoots the family and commits suicide. We can't figure out why. The answer is never simple. But too often there is no joy, no love, and the absence of caring by others as well as by the individual.

Depression is a very dangerous mental condition and often left untreated leads to suicide. Too often it is coupled with murder. There is a perverted sense that if things are that bad for the individual who is suffering then:

a. Everyone else must be feeling really bad too, or:
b. They have no right to feel so good when I feel so bad.

Depression for the sufferer is like a downward winding spiral staircase, and the further down the staircase the sufferer goes the faster the descent until rock bottom is hit. It is a black and gloomy experience. Most depressions that are left untreated result in deeper and darker bottoms.

It is at the point just after bottoming out that the depressed person is most likely to attempt suicide. It is the frustration and fear of the long climb back to level that makes the depressed person feel hopeless and unable to cope. It is here that the compassionate Christian needs to be sensitive and loving.

The late Dr. Raymond Brock asserted that there are three specific questions that must be asked of the depressed person, and if dealt with in a Biblical manner the answers will help alleviate the majority of symptoms in even the worst cases of depressions.

We must first note that there are two major types of depression and each must be diagnosed by a trained professional. We shall mention them here for clarity, one is medical in nature and is the result of a chemical imbalance in the body's system. This type can often be controlled with diet and medication. The other is psychological in nature and can be helped with counsel and nurturing. It is important to realize that there are many cases that involve both physical and psychological depressions. We must also note that psychological depression can lead to a chemical imbalance that then requires medical treatment to return to physical health as well as emotional health.

Let us now address Dr. Brock's three questions.
1. What are you afraid of?
2. What have you done that makes you feel guilty?
3. Who are you angry with or who do you hate?

As we examine each question we can quickly sense that the person with any of these feelings is not going to have much joy. Fear is a paralyzer, it gripes the mind and emotions and keeps us from functioning, and if it keeps us from loving it robs us of the opportunity for love, and hence joy.

If it keeps us from anything, such as flying in a plane, we get angry at our own inability to overcome the inanimate things of this world. Such self-directed anger keeps us from a healthy self-love that is vital to giving love that results in fullness of joy.

It is possible to feel fear and to have fears without allowing them to overcome us to the point where it hinders us, but the moment we are in the place or position that we are afraid our joy goes right out the window. In those times of fear, we must return to God's word and Joshua records one of the best

"Have I not commanded you? Be strong and courageous! Do not tremble or be dismayed, for the LORD your God is with you wherever you go."
Joshua 1:9 *NASB*

Isaiah has another excellent passage on fear.

But now, thus says the LORD, your Creator, O Jacob, And He who formed you, O Israel, "Do not fear, for I have redeemed you; I have called you by name; you are Mine! Isaiah 43:1 *NASB*

Guilt lets us know we have been separated from God. Right? Not always is this the total truth. satan uses guilt that is unrealistic to keep us at a place where we cannot feel the warmth of God's love. Guilt that is from God warns us that if we do not correct the situation that we will be in danger of eternal damnation, and this is healthy in the life of the believer.

Unrealistic guilt is the guilt that comes again and again over the same thing even though you know that you have taken it to the Lord and He has forgiven you. You have made it right with the one you offended if that was needed and yet you still feel massive loads of guilt. satan is working to destroy the joy of this believer.

If it is unresolved sin it will work to keep us from God and open the doors for depression based upon loss of relationship. If it is unrealistic guilt then it is the trick of the enemy to foil our joy by sending us into depression that is not necessary.

Who are you angry at is Brock's third question. We are warned in the Scriptures not to let the sun go down upon our wrath, yet we persist as people to do so. When we are still angry today about something that happened yesterday or before we have not followed the teachings of Paul the Apostle concerning being angry and sinning not.

Frederick Buechner writes in Wishful Thinking, A Theological ABC's[2]:

"Of the Seven Deadly Sins, anger is possibly the most fun. To lick your wounds, to smack your lips over grievances long past, to roll over your tongue the prospect of bitter confrontation still to come, to savor to the last toothsome morsel both the pain you are given and the pain you are giving back -- in many ways is a meal fit for a king. The chief drawback is that what you are wolfing down is yourself. The skeleton at the feast is you."

In the past couple of decades, we have moved to a position of "it is OK for Christians to get angry" from a position that said for so long that we are not allowed any anger. As we see more depression within the Christian community we must ask ourselves if in our haste to make it OK to get angry did we throw the baby out with the bath water? Have we really learned to dismiss our anger at the end of the day? Are we brooding over past disputes to the point we lose our joy and face depression?

I believe we have, and we need to return to a Biblical pattern of resolving the conflicts before the day ends, or getting on our face before God and turning the problem over to His control. We must let God be in control lest we become a generation of church people that know the forms of Godliness, but know not the joys of salvation.

Matthew Henry[3] wrote "Holy mourning makes for Holy Mirth" Is it time for the church to seek God to overcome fear, anger and guilt that joy might be restored once again? Yes, today and always. The New Testament admonishes us to turn our joy in to mourning, and to humble ourselves before God. We need the experience of seeing the neediness of our joy, and the turning of it into mourning as we realize the depth of His joy, and then to pursue the Joy of the Lord as we walk in the love that He has called us.

I hope you understand the need to be with the One who loves you even more than a parent, more than a brother, sister, child or spouse. If you want joy, you will need love. Without love can there truly be any joy?

JOY IN ACTION

If you are struggling with Joy in your life and have not yet done so, take time now to review Dr. Raymond Brock's three questions. Here they are again for your review:

1. What are you afraid of?
2. What have you done that makes you feel guilty?
3. Who are you angry with or Who do you hate?

FEAR

To begin the process of developing joy we must first begin to eliminate fear. As a youth pastor I was assigned the care of a lady in the church who lost her husband due to illness. At first, she was receptive to my visits. She was close to my grandmothers age, and I was in my 20's at the time. At first, she would greet me at the door and we would chat. As the weeks wore on, she got more reclusive. She was afraid every visitor was going to bring some dreaded disease into her home that would cause her to get sick and die. She developed full-blown agoraphobia. In case you are not familiar with the term, here is the Wikipedia definition:

> **Agoraphobia** is an anxiety disorder characterized by symptoms of anxiety in situations where the

person perceives their environment to be unsafe with no easy way to escape. These situations can include open spaces, public transit, shopping centers, or simply being outside their home. Being in these situations may result in a panic attack. The symptoms occur nearly every time the situation is encountered and last for more than six months. Those affected will go to great lengths to avoid these situations. In severe cases people may become completely unable to leave their homes.

Even as a Christian she allowed the fear to overcome her. At about this time a wonderful Psalm-song came into the church world. It is from Psalm 27 a favorite of mine. Here are a few verses. I strongly suggest reading them repeatedly if you have fear that is stealing your joy.

The LORD is my light and my salvation; Whom shall I fear? The LORD is the defense of my life; Whom shall I dread? When evildoers came upon me to devour my flesh, my adversaries and my enemies, they stumbled and fell. Though a host encamp against me, my heart will not fear; Though war arise against me, in spite of this I shall be confident.
Psalms 27:1-3 NASB

SCRIPTURES TO BATTLE FEAR

Genesis 15: 1	*Psalm 27: 1-3*
Exodus 14: 14	*Psalm 34: 1-4*
Deuteronomy 3: 22	*Psalm 42: 1-5*
Deuteronomy 31: 6	*Psalm 56: 3-4*
Joshua 1: 9	*Psalm 91: 1-16*
Psalm 23: 1-6	*Psalm 94: 16-19*

Psalm 118: 5-7	*Romans 8: 38-39*
Isaiah 41: 10-13	*Philippians 4: 6-7*
Isaiah 42: 1	*2 Timothy 1: 3*
Matthew10: 29-31	*Hebrews 13: 5-6*
Mark 6: 5-50	*I Peter 5: 5-7*
John 14: 27	*I John 4: 17-21*
Romans 8: 12-17	*Revelation 21: 4*

GUILT

Our second obstacle to joy is guilt. It seems every time I hear a preacher give an alter call I should put my hand in the air for I am standing right beside Paul when he declared he was foremost (chief in the King James) among sinners.

It is a trustworthy statement, deserving full acceptance, that Christ Jesus came into the world to save sinners, among whom I am foremost of all.
1 Timothy 1:15 NASB

Guilt is a real killjoy. As a Christian we must understand the dynamics of forgiveness. There is a wonderful book by Pastor Cecil Barham on the subject of The Dynamics of Forgiveness[4]. You will have to search for it, as it is not a huge selling book. As of this writing you can get it on Amazon.com. I can assure you this book can revolutionize your life in both receiving the forgiveness in your own life that can be illusive and in the giving of forgiveness that will come into play in a moment when we look at our third killjoy.

One thing about forgiveness I did not learn from Barham is that there is a lot of unrealistic guilt that besets the Christian. Unrealistic guilt is the trick of the enemy to make you lose your joy. Let me illustrate.

Several years ago, I was pastoring in a small rural Minnesota community. We were only an hour from the Twin Cities of Minneapolis and St. Paul. Everything we could need or want was within an hour's drive, yet we had the rural farm community in which to live. It was here that I met Jim. (Not his real name as I would not want to embarrass him at this late date. He did give me permission years ago to use his story, as it is an excellent example of unrealistic guilt.)

Jim stopped by the church one morning; I think it was a Thursday, to talk to me. He was a relatively young Christian in his mid-20's. He was anxious, as he had been struggling to overcome being an angry person. He had grown up knowing mostly drunken, and drug induced anger in his home on the part of one parent and he desperately wanted to break out of that mold and become a man of God.

We talked at length about some strategies for anger in a Biblical context. Things like praying for those who take advantage. Being angry and not sinning, and had a good time together as we explored the Word of God. We prayed for control and Jim left with a renewed sense of God in his life and with the knowledge that he would control his anger better in the future. He left to go to work in a neighboring community at a Big Box Store.

His ride to work was filled with joy. Until he got to the parking lot. There he spotted a parking place big enough for the old police interceptor he drove. As he politely allowed someone to drive out of his way before entering the spot a small foreign car (known at the time as a ricer) pulled into "his" spot. Got out and laughed at him in his big ugly retired cop car.

Jim nearly lost it all while he sought out another parking spot. As he told me about this later he was telling me some of the things that went through his mind at the time regarding what he was going to do to the driver of the ricer. He also told me of the check that came into his spirit, driven by the Holy Spirit, to bring that anger under the Holy Spirit's as control we had just talked about. He decided right then on his way into the store for his shift that he was not going to fall victim to the anger again. In those few moments he went from joy to anger and back to joy. But the story does not end here.

Fast forward to about six hours from our first meeting of the day. I am ready to leave the office, just clearing my desk from the day's work and study. Ready to go home to my family. Okay, we were empty nesters so it was my wife and the dog. The door to my office was ajar, suddenly it swings wide, and there is Jim, an emotional wreck.

I had never seen him in such a state. I had to ask, of course, what was wrong? He began to relate the tale I have just told, with this added. After he got into the store, the guilt was overwhelming. As I listened, I began to realize the subtlest trick of the enemy of your souls and mine.

Unrealistic guilt. You see Jim had been tempted to revert to his old ways of anger and retribution, but he stopped and prayed and got relief from the thoughts. The enemy, and just so no one thinks otherwise I am talking about satan himself; (I hate mentioning his name so I seldom do and I never capitalize a denotation to him. I prefer to think of him always as the enemy, never anything more. He is the destroyer and deserves no time or effort.) The enemy attacked this young man over having had the thoughts cross his mind that he could take some revenge on the driver of the other car.

All day long he struggled with the guilt of having let the thoughts even get into his head. He was tormented that he would never overcome the anger we had prayed so earnestly about that morning. He felt doomed to become the parent he despised and never become the person he wanted to become. The guilt was overwhelming his very being.

I did something that I have regretted many times since. I started to chuckle, and then to laugh. Poor Jim, he was taking all this so seriously and it was painful for him and then here I was laughing at him in his dilemma. I will tell you now he soon saw the humor and had a small laugh but I sure wish it had gone a little differently.

Here is why I laughed. Jim was being tormented for doing what all of us must do in times of temptation. He took the route of escape. He turned it over to the Lord Jesus Christ in a word of prayer and moved on to joy. The enemy just could not stand that Jim had joy in spite of the temptation so he tried to convince Jim that the temptation was the sin, not the acting out of the temptation.

I have met many people that are burdened with unrealistic guilt. Unrealistic guilt tells you, "you cannot be forgiven." That is correct, it is impossible to forgive yourself for something you did not actually commit. Other times it is an incomplete understanding of the tremendous grace that Jesus afforded us by His sacrificial death on the cross.

I have often made the claim that the strongest force in the universe is God's Grace. I say that without a thought to diminish the power of God in creation. I acknowledge the power of creation, but there is something about grace, that undeserved loving kindness of God toward His human creation. Here is why I make the claim. Creation cannot change a sinner into a saint. You cannot hug enough trees to accomplish it, eat enough bugs and plants, wash enough shorelines or do any other sort of penance in your search for redemption.

There is only one thing that can accomplish this transformation in all of the universe, the Grace of God, and it makes us clean and removes all stain and sets us free from guilt and shame. And it restores unto us the Joy of our Salvation.

PSALMS 51

For the choir director. A Psalm of David, when Nathan the prophet came to him, after he had gone in to Bathsheba.

Be gracious to me, O God, according to Your lovingkindness; According to the greatness of Your compassion blot out my transgressions. Wash me thoroughly from my iniquity and cleanse me from my sin. For I know my transgressions, and my sin is ever before me. Against You, You only, I have sinned and done what is evil in Your sight, so that You are justified when You speak and blameless when You judge. Behold, I was brought forth in iniquity, and in sin my mother conceived me. Behold, You desire truth in the innermost being, and in the hidden part You will make me know wisdom. Purify me with hyssop, and I shall be clean; Wash me, and I shall be whiter than snow. Make me to hear joy and gladness, Let the bones which You have broken *rejoice. Hide Your face from my sins and blot out all my iniquities. Create in me a clean heart, O God, and renew a steadfast spirit within me. Do not cast me away from Your presence and do not take Your Holy Spirit from me. **Restore to me the joy of Your salvation** and sustain me with a willing spirit.*

Psalms 51:1-12 NASB

SCRIPTURES TO BATTLE GUILT
NOT FEELING FORGIVEN

Nehemiah 9:17	*Acts 2:38*
Psalm 13:4	*Acts 5:31*
Daniel 9:9	*Acts 10:43*
Matthew 26:28	*Acts 13:38*
Mark 1:4	*Acts 26:18*
Luke 1:77	*Ephesians 1:7*
Luke_3:3	*Colossians 1:14*
Luke 27:47	*Hebrews 9:22*

ANGER

We come to Brocks third question. Who are you angry with, who do you hate?

In the last section Jim had cause to be angry, but we saw him overcome. Jim had a way to go, but he was on a good path from then on, today when I hear of him he is doing some amazing things with his life and I am grateful to have had a chance to know him and be a part of his life.

I wish that everyone could deal with anger so quickly, but it is a strong tool of the enemy to destroy joy. I hope you underlined Buechner's quote (page 42) about anger. If you did not go back and read it again and underline it. It is imperative that we understand who loses in anger and hatred.

Here are some Scriptures to meditate upon:

SCRIPTURES TO BATTLE ANGER

Exodus 34: 6

Number 14: 18

Nehemiah 9: 17

Psalm 6: 1

Psalm 30: 5

Psalm 37: 8

Psalm 86:15

Psalm 145: 8

Proverbs 14: 29

Proverbs 15: 1

Proverbs 16: 32

Proverbs 19: 11

Proverbs 22: 24

Proverbs 29: 8

Ecclesiastes 7: 9

Ecclesiastes 11: 10

Matthew 18: 34

Ephesians 4: 26

Ephesians 4: 31

Ephesians 6: 4

Colossians 3: 8

James 1: 19, 20

SCRIPTURES TO DISCOVER GOD'S JOY

The word joy is used 170 times in the New American Standard Bible. Generally, it speaks of the joy of God's people. In the following ten verses you will find the Joy of God described.

1 Chronicles 16:26-27   Psalms 51:12

Nehemiah 8:10   Ecclesiastes 2:26

Job 8:19   Zephaniah 3:17

Psalms 16:11   John 15:11

Psalms 43:4   John 17:13

CHAPTER FOUR

THE FRUIT OF PEACE

"Peace I leave with you; My peace I give to you; not as the world gives do I give to you. Do not let your heart be troubled, nor let it be fearful.
                                        John 14:27 NASB

The day will come upon this earth and indeed has come many times especially twice during this last century when all mankind has called out for peace. Pure peace is that one commodity that we all want, and yet never seem to enjoy. We talk about peace of mind, peace and quiet, peace and solitude, and peace on earth. Yet, we cannot get a moment's peace. We are looking for a peacemaker in our world, yet when we get one it seems we are all skeptical of that person's influence. We need only to look at current world conditions to see that we have a Russian leader who seemingly is working for world peace. In the late eighty's and early nineties, we had a U.S. President that did not want to spend the peace windfall on anything but more new weapons.

As I first wrote this in the late '80's I thought of a news report I heard where Nelson Mandela would not meet with Secretary of State James Baker III because he would meet with the South African President de Klerk, the leader who after 23 years arranged Mandela's freedom. Why? Because de Klerk and Mandela do not believe in the same brand of peace.

I want peace, you want peace, we all want peace and some are willing to give it all away to have peace. Peace at any cost, cry some of my peers, and others will defend to the death the rights they have rather than have peace of a foreign nature.

(Authors note: Since this was originally written we have had the Gulf War, a second Gulf war and constant tensions in the region including Syria, Afghanistan, etc., not to mention the increase of terrorism both at home and abroad. As a nation, some scream for gun control and others for more armed guards to insure peace. History will have to inform the reader of the outcomes of this conflict. December 26, 2018)

Where does it all end and how do we get some of God's wonderful peace?

PEACE AS AN ATTRIBUTE

For a child will be born to us, a son will be given to us; And the government will rest on His shoulders; And His name will be called Wonderful Counselor, Mighty God, Eternal Father, Prince of Peace. There will be no end to the increase of His government or of peace, On the throne of David and over his kingdom, to establish it and to uphold it with justice and righteousness from then on and forevermore. The zeal of the LORD of hosts will accomplish this.
Isaiah 9:6-7 NASB

Three hundred, two times the Scriptures refer to peace, 85 times, and only in the Old Testament, it refers to the peace offering. Andrew Jukes in *The Law of The Offerings* (page 106ff) points out that the peace offering was the only offering in which the priest and God were both fed.

He further goes on to show Christ as a participant in the offering and demonstrates the purity of the peace offering.

David wrote in the Psalms:

The LORD will give strength to His people; The LORD will bless His people with peace.
Psalms 29:11 NASB

Paul wrote in his first letter to the Thessalonians:

Now may the God of peace Himself sanctify you entirely; and may your spirit and soul and body be preserved complete, without blame at the coming of our Lord Jesus Christ. 1 Thessalonians 5:23 NASB

When we look into the Scripture we see a sincere and difficult dichotomy that puzzles the beginning student and the agnostic alike. The young student of God's Word looks at the text and cannot grasp the complexity of the ever-raging wars of the Old Testament, and asks why. The agnostic/atheist looks and says if there was a god and indeed he was a loving god as we Christians assert then this god must not be in control or else he is asleep at the wheel at times to allow such devastation of humanity as wars produce.

We preach a God of peace and yet the war rages in almost all of our literature. We, in the Christian community are obsessed with the war between good and evil. That certainly is not wrong or bad, but has the effect of tainting our credibility with the non-Christian world or the nominal, carnal Christian.

We are in good company when on the one hand we talk about peace and then stand up, ready to fight the war on pornography or abortion. Jesus, whom the angels heralded with such sayings as "Peace on earth, good will toward men" stunned His followers with this one day:

"Do not think that I came to bring peace on the earth; I did not come to bring peace, but a sword. "For I came to SET A MAN AGAINST HIS FATHER, AND A DAUGHTER AGAINST HER MOTHER, AND A DAUGHTER-IN-LAW AGAINST HER MOTHER-IN-LAW; and A MAN'S ENEMIES WILL BE THE MEMBERS OF HIS HOUSEHOLD."

Matthew 10:34-36 NASB

Is it any wonder our kids are sometimes confused, and the world thinks we are nuts?

Here is a God that gives the most amazing, the most desirable, and the most valuable sense of well-being known to mortal man, and then He comes off with a statement like that. He says that He will bring the sword and we pray for the unity of our families asking according to the Scripture that declares that we shall be saved and our household. Time and again we see God honor His word and families are reunited and the peace of God reigns in their homes.

We could go on and on exploring this dichotomy without bringing any conclusion to it, however, the answers are really quite simple even though there seems no sensible way to resolve this paradox. Our God is a God of Peace. Scripture declares that Jesus, His Son is the Prince of Peace. Jesus could not be the Prince if there was not a King, ergo, God himself becomes the King of Peace, as Jesus the Christ is the only begotten Son of God.

There is much more to God than just simple one-sidedness. He is also a Just and Holy God. He cannot tolerate sin in His presence, or any un-holiness. He will do just about anything at this time, and in times past, to squelch this present evil, short of totally destroying His creation. Yet, His word does teach that even this creation is slated for final destruction when all evil will be banished forever. Then and only then, we who are counted among the faithful, will receive benefit from the full expression of His Peace.

PEACE AS EMOTION

"The steadfast of mind You will keep in perfect peace, because he trusts in You. Isaiah 26:3 NASB

Thou wilt keep him in perfect peace, whose mind is stayed on thee: because he trusteth in thee.
Isaiah 26:3 KJV

I have chosen to use both KJV and NASB for this quote because of the nuances both bring to the table. NASB uses steadfast mind, the KJV the mind "stayed" on God. In the Hebrew the word is the same, it is the translator's thoughts that go into the translation of the word. When I see these two words my mind goes to James 1:8 and the double-mined man. I can have something "stayed" on my mind and be back and forth about what I shall do with the information I am pondering. Should I? Should I not? That battle rages in all of us from time to time. It can be associated with temptation as we battle with the enemy.

Steadfast to me goes a step further than "stayed." It denotes a direction is chosen and there is no turning back. The decision is made and it settled in heaven and earth and I shall keep my mind on the things of God. It is here that the potential for an emotional peace can begin.

When there is no peace there is turmoil, there are questions about everything that can be discovered. Fear can take control, as there is uncertainty about everything and everyone. Politicians feed the fears by declaring everything is bad. If you read anything about food and drink, you can find a study on just about everything that tells you it is bad for your health. This world operates on fear mongering. Emotions run high at the very mention of political and social issues, and there is no peace for both sides of the issue.

Because of this dynamic, the only place peace can be found is in the mind that is steadfast on the things of God.

A great exercise when feeling depressed or despondent is the reading of the Psalms. They will bring peace to the troubled heart, and in reading them the reader begins to focus the mind on the things of God. When the mind is steadfast on God, His Word, and our relationship to Him through the Son, peace can return.

You can use the chart in Addendum A to read the Psalms in 30 days. At the end of each day's readings, try to discover three things to focus your mind on regarding your relationship with God.

Finding a stable emotional peace will come when God's Word is at the center of your thinking. There are thousands of verses with promise in the Bible. A very significant one that speaks to our peace is found in Timothy:

> *For God hath not given us the spirit of fear; but of*
> *power, and of love, and of a sound mind.*
> 2 Timothy 1:7 KJV

When our peace is destroyed, fear comes in. When we recognize the beauty of Paul's word's to Timothy we can begin to see the fear lift, and Peace return. We must make the decision to seek God's Word, and to seek out a stronger relationship with Jesus the Son to see our peace strengthened and developed.

THE LINK OF LOVE IN PEACE

Let us move on to consider the relationship of love to the fruit of Peace. We are very aware at this time of the fact that God is the God of Peace, the God of true Joy, and that God is Love. Our need now is to demonstrate both from Scripture and life, the need for love to exist for peace to be present.

> *What is the source of quarrels and conflicts among you? Is not the source your pleasures that wage war in your members? You lust and do not have; so, you commit murder. You are envious and cannot obtain; so, you fight and quarrel. You do not have because you do not ask. You ask and do not receive, because you ask with wrong motives, so that you may spend it on your pleasures.*   James 4:1-3 NASB

What a huge indictment of the human condition. If we were to look into history for very long we would see the correlation between verse one and virtually every war that has ever been fought, including the crusades. It has always been that you have something that I want, and I will treat you badly until you surrender it or I take it from you.

You do not have to start the war for the war to rage, you just have to be part of the war. The battle for your very soul is found in the enemy wanting to control you. The battles of temptation, the enemy wants to control your soul. The battle with your spouse, the enemy wants to control your marriage to destroy it. Sometimes it is our lusts and greed that start the war, sometimes it is imposed upon us, to our dismay.

No matter how the battles begin, if we get caught up in them, our peace is destroyed. Paul wrote about this when writing to the Corinthians. Perhaps the most poignant verse is this one.

> *(Love) ...does not act unbecomingly; it does not seek its own, is not provoked, does not take into account a wrong suffered,*   1 Corinthians 13:5 NASB

We realize that our world is on the brink of war with every news report. There is yet a greater concern that I wish to address here and that is the warring that goes on in the church in the name of God. For peace to exist then love must be both present and demonstrated by the body of Christ. As we have come into the Twenty-First century it has become fashionable in some circles of the church world to attack every other ministry that is not totally affiliated with yours.

Mega-church, multi-campus Pastors have become super stars in the church world and their every word is scrutinized for some slight area where people can disagree. Let me note that some criticisms are warranted, but some are just plain nick-picking to cause strife. I go back to James when he states the wars are the result of lust. The thinking must be something along the lines of "I want the money, prestige, people you have." Nothing else seems to make sense and it is rooted in the work of the enemy to destroy peace in the church.

The only solution is for love to be applied. I will not act unbecomingly toward my fellow Christians. I may disagree, and it is important to scholarly pursuit of the whole truth of God's Word for debate to take place. However, there is a very Biblical principle for dealing with conflict that needs to be applied when the debate becomes a battle. Check it out in Matthew 18: 15-18

Love thinks no evil, love is caring, compassionate, interested in and above all concerned about the needs of others. We said when we talked of joy that to make the statement that joy only comes from the acrostic of Jesus, Others, you, was incorrect. Yet, love will always, when it operates in a healthy environment, include an outward reaching, Christian ready to share the peace and love that comes only from Christ Jesus.

Love does not seek her own way. Romans 12:10 teaches us that with honor we are to prefer one another or in other words with honor we should set others wishes before ours. As mature Christians we must also realize that we cannot, to operate in love, compromise the gospel just so we don't have a war or un-peaceful situation on our hands.

We must heed what Paul writes in Romans 14 not to include the weak and new Christian in discussions about Scripture and doctrine that is divisive. I believe that he said this because even mature Christians tend to shoot their mouth off now and then and need to ask one another for forgiveness. We must, however, not try to spiritualize foolishness.

You may have heard of church splits over the song book to be purchased, the color of the new carpet, and a half dozen other pathetic items of foolishness. I actually know of a church that split in the 1970's over the color of the new song books. Some wanted red to represent the blood of Christ, the other half of the church wanted white to represent the purity of Salvation. The battle was settled with dividing the church. Most often if you talk with one of the members of the church you will find that they feel they are contending for doctrinal purity on some issue, and that is why they split, (to that I usually say, "Hogwash").

It is because people are not walking as they should walk, emulating the love of God. They are walking as they want, not as God would direct, and as a result they behave unseemly. I can just guess that you know who it is I am talking about, or at least someone like who I am talking about. Who I am talking about is you and I. We get so caught up in our pet projects that we fail to look at the sum of the whole and only see our little part, causing tainted vision that leads to war.

It may not be fisticuffs (although that has happened more than once in the church), but it becomes a war of words, dirty looks, un-kept promises (those always work real good to make someone else looks foolish), and even if others do take sympathy because they know it is not their fault, they still look foolish for having let you be the one responsible, and on and on it goes. Words, deeds, and attitudes is what destroys the very essence of our faith. We say things like, "I can't worship in the same church as so and so," "or I just wish they would go somewhere else so that we can have some peace around here." All of this just adds to the war, and the peace is destroyed.

I once was a candidate for a church that had three men come for a try out, we each came for a weekend and we all had similar qualifications for the job. I had perhaps a little more education but as far as job experience we were about equal, which is where the difference ended. One was very youth orientated, one the more traditional service mind set (me) and the third was very much into the charismatic worship style. The church was about 80% middle age but some were very interested in the charismatic style of worship and held the majority vote in the congregation. It was a slim margin to be sure. The problem began when the majority of the board wanted me, but the majority of the pulpit committee wanted the other man. Here was where the war began, a war that ended with a split, not over doctrine, not over anything important, but over nothing other than the personality of the new, yet un-hired, pastor. This was not love in action. It was self-serving egotism. It is hard to realize that a church split over an unknown.

Never pay back evil for evil to anyone. Respect what is right in the sight of all men. If possible, so far as it depends on you, be at peace with all men. Never take your own revenge, beloved, but leave room for the wrath of God, for it is written, "VENGEANCE IS MINE, I WILL REPAY," says the Lord. "BUT IF YOUR ENEMY IS HUNGRY, FEED HIM, AND IF HE IS THIRSTY, GIVE HIM A DRINK; FOR IN SO DOING YOU WILL HEAP BURNING COALS ON HIS HEAD." Do not be overcome by evil, but overcome evil with good. Romans 12:17-21 NASB

Love says "I will heap coals of fire upon the head of my enemy by having compassion upon him, I will give him a drink when he thirsts, and I will feed him when he is hungry." (Romans 12:20 my paraphrase)

Giving coals on the head is not to burn the subject it is to provide a needed commodity for the heating and cooking needs of the home. Today you could change this to bringing a full 6 course meal to the home of your enemy complete with appetizer, desert and a thermos of coffee or some other appropriate beverage.

The coals of fire that this brings, is the guilt and the shame of your love for them even when they are un-lovely. The next verse says be not overcome with evil but overcome evil with good. (Romans 12:21)

Peace in the Christian walk is to me the state of existence that comes from fulfilling the law of Christ toward our brothers and sisters. Paul wrote in Romans 12:17 "that we were to recompense no man evil for evil," or more simply don't pay the other guy back for what he did to you.

With exceptions, most wars in the church get started because so in so got slighted by Mr. or Mrs. Pufpofnick (insert any real names here for your own amusement) and then begins to hold a grudge, begins to devise ways to pay back the Pufpofnick's and before too long there is a full-scale church war going on. Why?

Because we think more highly than we ought to think of ourselves, and then we work something unseemly and then we have war, and no peace in our life. We scheme and scheme and then expect God to give us peace. We should not be so ignorant of the devil's devices.

Paul said (Romans 12:19) "don't take your own revenge" simply because God is keeping track of things, He will defend you and take care of you. You do not have to be someone's door mat getting stepped on all the time. You have the freedom to move out of the way. Just remember to let God take care of the vengeance. Show the "Love of Christ" instead of your human anger.

I wish I was a better example of this so I could gloat all over these pages of how wonderful I am at it, but let me tell you this a journey we all have to travel. It is a difficult journey and you will falter and fail from time to time. I welcome you to join in the process. I also welcome you to adopt the attitude of Dorotheos[1] the sixth century monk who said "we fall down, we get up, we fall down we get up." We don't need to get into the fray with others over our own personal well-being, if we are truly willing to give Christ Jesus the place He deserves in our Lives.

Secondly, Paul writes in verse 18 "If possible, so far as it depends on you, be at peace with all men." This is a big challenge for us all, to live peaceably with all men. There are days when we all let a little Jackie Gleason out. Do you remember that immortal scene when Gleason doubles his fist and utters those memorable words "to the moon Alice, to the moon". They often come when nothing else is going favorably for us. But, we cannot let our peace be destroyed by circumstances, we must learn contentment because satan is out to destroy your peace, with wars and rumors of war.

Let us turn our attention now to those wars and rumors of wars and the effects of no peace on our daily lives. By destroying our peace, the enemy of our souls can leave us in dire straits full of discontent and fear. I read some years ago that often under fire in the battle fields of any war that fear of the outcome, death, and injury can be so great that even the bravest of men will have the experience of having their bowels and bladder lose control. They will soil themselves without any ability to control the situation. This fact is just dealt with as "a matter of fact" and no one gets too excited or comments about the experience.

I mention it now simply to show the great intensity of fear, and its effect on the human body. War causes fear. Fear destroys at a very slow pace the emotional stability of the person. Fear consumes the mind and paralyzes the individual.

There is a psychological disorder (agoraphobia, see fear in chapter 3 for more discussion on this) that causes so much fear that the sufferer will not leave the protection of their own home. (There have been several TV specials on this subject in the past.) Such intense fear is not what God intended man to live under when He gave us the ability to sense danger and to walk with a certain amount of caution. Caution such as one would experience when traversing the narrow paths along the edge of a ravine. That healthy emotion out of control becomes the weapon of satan to paralyze the church. That fear keeps you from sharing the gospel lest you get ridiculed. It keeps us from reaching out to others for fear of being an intrusion in their life. In general, fear paralyzes and leaves us feeling guilty and destroys the peace that should be ours as a fruit of the Spirit.

So, we need to fight back with Scripture and an understanding of what God's Word says.

For God has not given us the spirit of fear but of power, and of love and of a sound mind.
II Timothy 1:7 KJV

What a beacon of hope for those who suffer from psychological disorders this verse can be and has been. It also has been used as a Scriptural whipping post for those who do suffer from psychological disorders. I am convinced, that Paul wrote this for us as a light shining in the darkness for those who struggle from time to time with inordinate psychological disorders and mental health diseases. The enemy would use this to whip the saint who is struggling, and entices those who don't to belittle and put down, instead of lifting up and supporting those who have such difficulties, as we need to do for our brothers and sisters.

Paul also wrote to the church in Corinth:

God is not the author of confusion but of peace as in all the churches of the saints.
I Corinthians 14:33 KJV

We must be careful here not to do injustice to the text by ignoring its placement. Here Paul is writing about the ministry of the Holy Spirit in the local church. We can clearly see that God is the author of peace in the church. The enemy would destroy that peace by getting men to war one with another causing confusion and strife.

James dispenses his wisdom concerning this by writing:

And the fruit of righteousness is sown in peace of them that make peace.   James 3:18 KJV

Peace then becomes both the nature of God's plan for the church and a measure of the maturity of the church's righteousness. Jesus put it this way:

Blessed are the peacemakers: for they shall be called the children of God.   Matthew 5:9 KJV

A lack of peace will produce in us nervousness, tension, worry, confusion, restlessness, fretting, wars, rumors of war and any number of other symptoms that destroy the Christian. God's gift to us is His peace. Check out these verses of Scripture:

The LORD will give strength to His people; The LORD will bless His people with peace.
Psalms 29:11 NASB

Those who love Your law have great peace, and

nothing causes them to stumble.
Psalms 119:165 NASB

Isaiah speaks of the perfect peace that we can experience when we focus our lives upon God:

> *"The steadfast of mind You will keep in perfect peace, because he trusts in You.*   Isaiah 26:3 NASB

Real lasting peace comes from a living relationship with Jesus Christ. It is part of what the Holy Spirit produces in us as we grow in the grace and knowledge of our Lord Jesus Christ.

Here are some faithful sayings to claim in the midst of a struggle where your peace is being challenged:

TRUTHS TO REMEMBER IN THE BATTLE FOR PEACE

The Lord fights for me; He has got this:

> *'You need not fight in this battle; station yourselves, stand and see the salvation of the LORD on your behalf, O Judah and Jerusalem.' Do not fear or be dismayed; tomorrow go out to face them, for the LORD is with you."*   2 Chronicles 20:17 NASB

I am a child of God:

> *The Spirit Himself testifies with our spirit that we are children of God, and if children, heirs also, heirs of God and fellow heirs with Christ, if indeed we suffer with Him so that we may also be glorified with Him.*   Romans 8:16-17 NASB

No weapon formed against me will be successful:

"No weapon that is formed against you will prosper; And every tongue that accuses you in judgment you will condemn. This is the heritage of the servants of the LORD, and their vindication is from Me," declares the LORD.   Isaiah 54:17 NASB

God is able to get me through and deal with this:

"For nothing will be impossible with God."
                                        Luke 1:37 NASB

His grace is sufficient:

And He has said to me, "My grace is sufficient for you, for power is perfected in weakness." Most gladly, therefore, I will rather boast about my weaknesses, so that the power of Christ may dwell in me.
                                        2 Corinthians 12:9 NASB

Christ has overcome the world and I can glory in His victory as He fights for me:

"These things I have spoken to you, so that in Me you may have peace. In the world you have tribulation, but take courage; I have overcome the world."
                                        John 16:33 NASB

Be still and know that He is God and He has this:

"Cease striving and know that I am God; I will be exalted among the nations, I will be exalted in the earth."   Psalms 46:10 NASB

SCRIPTURES TO RENEW YOUR PEACE

Numbers 25:12

Judges 6:24

Psalms 29:11

Psalms 37:37

Psalms 85:8, 10

Psalms 119:165

Psalms 122:6

Ecclesiastes 3:8

Isaiah 9:6, 7

Isaiah 26:3, 12

Isaiah 32:17

Isaiah 48:22

Isaiah 52:7, 12

Isaiah 54:10

Isaiah 60:17

Isaiah 66:12

Jeremiah 14:13

Jeremiah 33:6

Ezekiel 34:25

Ezekiel 37:26

Micah 5:5

Haggai 2:9

Zechariah 8:19

Malachi 2:5

Mark 9:50

John 14:27

John 16:33

Romans 5:21

Romans 8:6

Romans 12:18

Romans 14:17 – 19

Romans 15:33

I Corinthians 14:33

2 Corinthians 13:11

Ephesians 2:14 – 17

Philippians 4:9

Colossians 1:20

2 Thessalonians 3:16

2 Timothy 2:22

Hebrews 12:14

James 3:18   *1 Peter 3:11*

CHAPTER FIVE

THE FRUIT OF LONG-SUFFERING/PATIENCE

It almost seems unnecessary to approach the subject of the longsuffering/patience of God. Particularly this is true for the Christian, because the regenerated soul understands the patience with which God waited for their personal surrender to His call of salvation.

Patience and Long-suffering are used interchangeably more often than not. I use it this way, but as I write I think about the subtle differences in the two terms. I can be patient in waiting for a package, for my grandchildren to learn a math concept or grow up enough to understand a principle I want to teach them. I might struggle with patience when dealing with more complex issues in life such as a company overcharging me month by month and not being able to get the problem resolved.

If I suffer during these times it is usually due to my uncontrolled anger. See Fredrick Buechner's quote in chapter three again for the message he gives on anger. But there are times when the patience is painful. Just a few that come to mind are waiting for your prodigal child to return to the fold of Christ and family. I have been blessed not to experience this with my own children, but I have seen it many times in the lives of church people. The marriage that is falling apart, and one spouse is praying desperately for a miracle, while the other is praying (or just seeking) for the marriage to end. Then there is the pain of a chronic disease that never ends and eventually will take the life of the sufferer.

We might argue the last one on a purely empirically level as to whether it constitutes long suffering in the sense of patience, but my life experiences would indicate to me that unless you have experienced a long-term illness such as I am considering, your understanding may not be the same as mine. When you are in constant pain it is very difficult not to let your pain control who you are or your emotional responses.

With this introduction to Patience/Long-suffering here is our plan for this fruit's study:

Within this portion of our study we will show that:

1. God is Long-suffering.
2. Why God waits so patiently for us.
3. How we should walk and live in the light of Scripture in the area of patience.
4. Show how satan would delight and does delight in our lack of patient understanding and willingness to wait for an answer from God.
5. Share some quotes about Patience from history.

Let us now turn our attention to the Scripture and discover this attribute of God.

PATIENCE AS AN ATTRIBUTE

The LORD descended in the cloud and stood there with him as he called upon the name of the LORD. Then the LORD passed by in front of him and proclaimed, "The LORD, the LORD God, compassionate and gracious, slow to anger, and abounding in lovingkindness and truth; who keeps lovingkindness for thousands, who forgives iniquity, transgression and sin; yet He will by no means leave the guilty unpunished, visiting the iniquity of fathers on the children and on the grandchildren to the third and fourth generations." Exodus 34:5-7 NASB

Our first glimpse of the long-suffering of God comes when Moses is on Mount Sinai, Exodus 34:6, where God proclaims Himself merciful, gracious, long-suffering (KJV) or slow to anger, and abounding in loving kindness, truth, keeping mercy for thousands, forgiving iniquity, transgression and sin.

We talk about patience, and we express it by our very actions of impatience in our everyday lives. If you were a little late leaving your house this morning, no doubt you added a couple miles per hour to your personal speed limit and made up a couple of minutes in the process of getting to your destination. You may have even tried that new short-cut you found just to see if you could save a little by beating the old record time. You may have had any number of instant breakfast foods, and perhaps used a microwave oven to heat something. No doubt you will use such a device for the preparation of your noon meal, (unless of course you go out to a fast food restaurant where, if they don't serve you in two minutes or less, you will be angry and proclaim "what is taking so long!")

We live in a society that wants instant everything, and we want it to be as good as the real thing mom made. We compromise a lot just to get it quick. When computers first came out I personally didn't like computer type because it didn't look as nice aa a typewriter. Yet, in the interest of time the original of this book was computer generated on a dot matrix printer. In those days it was a very good one but, I had at my disposal two typewriters that would print from my computer, but I didn't want to take the time to setup the program to use them, and besides they were not as fast at printing out the final paper. Today I have printers that print several pages a minute and a computer that is perhaps more than 100,000 times faster and it is still too slow. I am just not very patient over some things.

But God is. Numbers finds Moses reminding God of all the things that He is:

> 'The LORD is slow to anger and abundant in lovingkindness, forgiving iniquity and transgression; but He will by no means clear the guilty, visiting the iniquity of the fathers on the children to the third and the fourth generations.'
>
> Numbers 14:18 NASB

Take a moment and refer back to the passage from Exodus 34:7 above for a parallel passage.

I have included here the final statement of this verse because it will give us another glimpse into the patience of God "...by no means clearing the guilty, visiting the iniquity of the fathers upon the children and the children's children to the third and fourth generation." He is willing to wait for repentance unto the third and fourth generations, and willing to carry the iniquity with its results three and four generations

We see everything in relationship to our personal life in years, God sees it in relationship to eternity. Perhaps the most impatient are the young, and as we grow we realize that we can wait a little while, (not too long mind you). We learn from society only one principle, that we can have it now. We have credit cards, loans, instant financing, etc., and we only subvert the growth of the individual, in developing patience. If you are wondering why your kids can't seem to wait for anything, look at the messages you and I are giving them by our lives, and realize they have only the experience of a few years where you and I have the experience of time.

The Psalmist writes:

> *But thou, O Lord, art a God full of compassion, and gracious, long-suffering, and plenteous in mercy and truth.* Psalm 86:15 KJV

Notice if you will that in all three of our references so far, we see long-suffering aligned with other qualities of God, such as compassionate, gracious, plenty of mercy and truth. In Exodus the same words, in Numbers we see forgiving of iniquity and transgression. A pattern has developed for us as we look at these Scriptures. We shall digress enough here to note that in addition to love, as we shall later show, compassion, mercy, graciousness, truth and forgiveness are all outward expressions of patience. We must practice patience with these other qualities or we won't see patience.

For nearly thirteen years I traveled the United States as a Minister under appointment to the American Bible Society. In my travels I regularly visited the missions of my territory, and I saw the generosity of a community displayed for all mankind to observe. Some states and communities provide very well for their poor and indigent. They have newer buildings that are clean and pleasant, and the staff is friendly and clean. In other locals the opposite is true, the buildings are run down, the staff is generally dressed such that you are not able to distinguish who is who. In the neat clean places, the people I worked with cared about their ministry to the poor with a sense of compassion. On the other hand, in the other missions there is a constant attitude that they must first change to come here, that we give them too much, no one cares about us, etc. (These are just general observations not necessarily 100% accurate in every case)

When all these qualities are brought together we get a glimpse of the patience in men. I know that those who exhibit the qualities of patience will be there to look for those who would come to Christ.

> *Or do you think lightly of the riches of His kindness and tolerance and patience, not knowing that the kindness of God leads you to repentance?*
> Romans 2:4 NASB

Romans 2:4 lets us see God again in the light of His patient long-suffering, Paul here writes to the Jews that it was the long-suffering of God coupled with His goodness and forbearance that was designed to lead the Jew to God via repentance. Paul is keenly aware of the difference an example will make. The old saying about "I complained about not having shoes until I saw the man who had no feet" rings true as to the power of this example.

How often have we seen in another a quality of mercy that we try to emulate? Or have we not said after we lost our patience over a situation, when upon hearing of another that they had endured a similar problem to the end said something like "well maybe, just maybe I jumped the gun a little bit"

By example God sought to lead the Jew to repentance and by example today He still seeks to lead us to repentance. He gave all that He had for our salvation, and He waits for us to make the decision to accept salvation. I Peter gives us an example of this very concept.

"For it is better, if God should will it so, that you suffer for doing what is right rather than for doing what is wrong. For Christ also died for sins once for all, the just for the unjust, so that He might bring us to God, having been put to death in the flesh, but made alive in the spirit; in which also He went and made proclamation to the spirits now in prison, who once were disobedient, when the patience of God kept waiting in the days of Noah, during the construction of the ark, in which a few, that is, eight persons, were brought safely through the water.

1 Peter 3:19-20 NASB

God is long-suffering and has a great love for His creation. Peter again gives us a glimpse of this love in 2 Peter 3:9

"The Lord is not slow about His promise, as some count slowness, but is patient (longsuffering KJV) toward you, not wishing for any to perish but for all to come to repentance." 2 Peter 3:9 NASB

In our search for growth it is always an exciting time when we begin to develop patience. No matter how old or young when we see the need for greater patience we also experience the unwanted but vital trying of our patience to develop that fruit in our lives. We struggle before God with the notion that we somehow are a failure if we are unable immediately to demonstrate the level of growth we think we should have. So, for these and many other situations let me give you a quotation from the book *Half Wits* by Gerald Goggins[1]:

"God does not depend on us...We depend upon Him."

Keep this in mind whenever you are faced with a trying situation. You will fare much better, you will go through the tough times with less battle scars, and less self-guilt. The key factor is of course to depend upon God in the mist of the trial.

PATIENCE AS EMOTION

I want it and I want it right now! If I do not get my way I will hold my breath until I do! The scene is from a children's movie, Willy Wonka's Chocolate Factory or Charlie and the Chocolate Factory either rendition, it does not matter. The children, except for Charlie are spoiled and demanding their rights, right now. It always reminds me I can be just like them.

Step out of the movie, and look around you at the world we live in. Check out the viral videos of the week and you are bound to see someone demanding their way. It starts at the presidency, flows through the congress, is legislated in the courts and spills out onto "reality" TV. In 2020 turn your TV on mid-day and between the court TV shows and the confrontational, tear the hair out, slap somebody down, gladiators performing for the cameras you might notice something.

The emotional response of a lack of patience. A popular commercial says "it's my money and I need cash now." To get that money you give up as much as fifteen percent of your principle. It might be the right thing to do in a financial crisis, but what if it is to fulfil a desire or lust? Then it has become about feeding the emotion of desire and not feeding the Biblical response of patience.

Paul wrote to the Romans:

But put on the Lord Jesus Christ, and make no provision for the flesh in regard to its lusts.
Romans 13:14 NASB

When we practice impatience, we are feeding our own desires. We have a desire that turns into a lust that we cannot contain and we have to have whatever it is, whether a new car or a new house. Popular TV shows at the time of this writing portray couples at odds over the home they have and one or the other person insisting on getting their own way. The battles between the spouses are so severe at times you wonder if they are headed to divorce court instead of a new home.

I want my way and I want it now has become the theme song of a present generation. Children demand certain things from their parents, and mom and dad in a deluded state of what is required to be a good parent give them what they demand. Teaching patience is narrowed to a five minute or less window. Temper tantrums at all ages reign supreme, and the emotional outbursts over getting it my way are over the top.

Patience is an emotional response to the stimulus of wanting something, whether good or bad. We are either patient, or we practice the antithesis.

PATIENCE'S ANTITHESIS

Is impatience the antithesis of Patience? Yes, and maybe no. I must admit it is an antithesis, but I also think there might just be more to the story. Here are a few quick thoughts on the Lack of Patience:

1. It shows a lack of faith.
2. It is a lack of understanding God's Word.
3. It is most likely a selfish act.
4. It can be childish in an adult.

Let me consider each of the above:

1. It shows a lack of faith because I do not trust God to work it out according to His plan. I jump into the fray because I cannot wait for God to act.

2. It is a lack of understanding Romans 8:28. God has declared that all things will work for the good of those who love Him, and it totally misses this important verse from Numbers

> *"God is not a man, that He should lie, nor a son of man, that He should repent; Has He said, and will He not do it? Or has He spoken, and will He not make it good?*
> Numbers 23:19 NASB

3. It is selfish. The lack of patience demands that the other people involved operate on your schedule. That is not always possible. In business you may need to be a bit more aggressive and it is not selfish, but if your issue is with another person and their inability to function at a particular level, your selfish attitude can be getting in the way of their growth. The demands you make may actually be keeping them from growing.

4. It can be childish in an adult. Open up your computer and visit a social media site. Spend a little time looking at the posted videos and you will see people having melt downs over all types of injustices, real and imagined. You will see a childish behavior by adults that is appalling. I don't need to say anymore. If you don't understand this point, please put this book away for a later date.

THE LOVE CONNECTION TO PATIENCE

Having said all of this let us now return our attention to the topic of Long-suffering and its relationship to us and love.

I Corinthians 13:4 states "Love suffers long and is kind;" Webster describes suffer this way: "to submit to or be forced to endure (martyrdom) b. to feel keenly: labor under 2 undergo, experience 3. to put up with especially as inevitable or unavoidable."

Long-suffering is all of that, and is often unavoidable because God uses the time to develop character in our lives. Consider, if you will this passage:

> Love... *bears all things, believes all things, hopes all things, endures all things.*
> 1 Corinthians 13:7 NASB

When we are in the place of having to learn, or demonstrate long-suffering we are also often going to find the need of a lot of faith and to take a lot on faith. There will certainly be times in the process of raising children through the teen years that will necessitate a little bearing of the weight of being patient in the throes of deep prayer. There will be times when you will have to trust your child even though you know they aren't giving you all the information you want. You will have to believe, and believe in, that child, even when you want to doubt. And in the process, you will need hope. Robert Schuler paraphrased President Franklin D. Roosevelt[2] when he said "hope is the rope in which you tie the knot until you can cope." When you have love, you can have patience, with patience you can develop hope and with hope, you can endure until the end.

A good friend of mine and a mentor for more than 40 years, Rev. John Otto, said to me once that he had yet to see a 25 to 28-year-old that hadn't gotten their life straightened around, no matter how bad they were, when they had received love and patience from both of their parents. He is in his 90's now so I guess he can make that kind of statement without too much contradiction. The key here is both parents. Many are the adults that are running around who did not have long-suffering, patient love from their fathers, and in some cases their mothers today. The results have become devastating to our society. All too often it is the father who loses his patience and damages the relationship. Dad's let us learn the lesson of patience so that we are not destroying our children. Patience waits, and waits, and waits, while providing Godly instruction, for the other person to develop and grow. Check out this verse if you have any doubt I am wrong:

Fathers, do not provoke your children to anger, but bring them up in the discipline and instruction of the Lord. Ephesians 6:4 NASB

It is necessary that patience is an example in all areas of life if you want change to take place in a person that is offensive toward you. You don't influence people, whom you must wait patiently for, by not showing them patience, along with the other fruits of the Spirit as they are in your life and developing in your life. You are the book they are reading to learn the skills you want them to have emulating from their life. If you don't have a manual it is very hard to repair a car, to fly a plane, to repair a computer, etc. You have to have a manual. In the case of the church and Christian development our manual is the Bible.

For the new or immature Christian there is a supplemental manual, the older Christian. The challenge is we are not necessarily wiser Christians. You and I must show love when they are unlovely. You and I must show peace when they are in turmoil. You and I must show patience when they are acting immature and demanding satisfaction now. You and I must be mature enough to help them develop as Godly men and women. We do that with love and the Fruit of the Spirit active in our lives.

In a section entitled *"Peace with God Through Faith"*, the New American Standard Bible records this passage

> *Therefore, having been justified by faith, we have peace with God through our Lord Jesus Christ, through whom also we have obtained our introduction by faith into this grace in which we stand; and we exult in hope of the glory of God. And not only this, but we also exult in our tribulations, knowing that tribulation brings about perseverance; and perseverance, proven character; and proven character, hope; and hope does not disappoint, because the love of God has been poured out within our hearts through the Holy Spirit who was given to us.* Romans 5:1-5 NASB

Paul the Apostle demonstrates in this passage that tribulation or trials give patience, and patience gives hope. He further demonstrates that hope is not something to be ashamed of, and it all comes about because of the LOVE of God poured into our lives. We will never develop our true capacity for growing the Fruit of the Spirit until we are willing to love unconditionally. Real love is tough because it demands maturing. But demands cannot be made until there is evidence of something to follow. For example, you can't say to your children, "you must be responsible with your money," unless you show them fiscal responsibility. You will not be able to teach them about love unless they feel loved.

I once had a friend whose father was into everything as a means to make money. In the process of that he made many unwise investments. He was not a bad man, and in many respects, he was a very generous Christian, with a generosity of time, talent, and wisdom. He gave of himself freely in as many ways as he possibly could, but he was not a good money manager. His son is a very generous committed Christian adult, giving of himself in time talent, and wisdom, but he is not a very good money manager, and like his father before him he tends to buy stuff he doesn't really need. The example his father gave left a lasting impression that affected a second generation. So too, the examples you give and leave on the life of your children will come through in the manner in which they live their lives.

Let us realize the reason for the trial is to teach us something, and in the process, to demonstrate to others the growth process and the love that is at the root of all of this fruit. We must realize that God loves us and gave us His love and by so doing He allows us to be in situations that make us grow up. Because of His love we go through the tough times.

An interesting parallel to this passage is the army training camp. They don't want their solders to get killed so they put them through such a rigorous training that recruits think they are going to die. In the end it is the training that will save their life. So, it is with tribulations, you think you can't make it, but in the end, you always learn about patience, the difficult part is application.

Be devoted to one another in brotherly love; give preference to one another in honor; not lagging behind in diligence, fervent in spirit, serving the Lord; rejoicing in hope, persevering in tribulation, devoted to prayer, Romans 12:10-12 NASB

We are interested in part of verse twelve from the above passage, persevering in tribulation. What a powerful statement. We all have tribulations, too often we want to be the one to fix the tribulation rather than persevere. What do your prayers sound like in the midst of a trial? "Oh, God, get me out of this trial," or "Father, teach me and have your perfect will in my life, develop in me your purpose and your fruit."

We often pray the first, but we need to pray the second. Rev. Otto put it this way years ago. "Sometimes because of our prayers God fixes the fix we are in, but we don't get fixed so God has to fix a bigger fix to get us fixed." Trials and tribulations are for the maturing of the saints. Maybe that explains why the more mature we are, the bigger the trial and the more grace we have to handle the trial. We can take it because of the smaller growth areas we had, or we can't take it because we short changed our development.

There are two ways to develop great big muscles, and as a result there are two types of muscular athletes, some have short muscles, and others have long muscles. Short muscle is often the body builder, the long muscle the strong man competitor. The short muscles come from one type of work out, considered by strong man competitors to be cheating on the work out, the long ones come slower and take longer to build but they have more elasticity. The long muscle comes from taking a completely different type of workout very seriously. Short muscle will tear more often, it does not have the strength of long muscles.

Therefore, when faced with a test of strength, short muscles will always lose, the long muscle that came over a longer period of time, by patient complete workouts will stand up to the testing of the muscle.

Tribulations are much the same. We don't get the full value by short cutting a trial. In the end we won't have the ability to withstand the big test. Rejoice, Paul said about trials, it builds up your faith and your fruit.

The writer of the Book of James also comments about this very same concept, so let us take a look at James:

> *Consider it all joy, my brethren, when you encounter various trials, knowing that the testing of your faith produces endurance.* James 1:2-3 NASB

James inserts the testing by temptations into his text. Let us not neglect the fact from God's word that temptation is also a maturing of our faith. Let me illustrate: several years ago, I wanted a new computer, one that had a regular keyboard, and had a modem so I could contact my office and leave electronic mail for my secretary. There were other reasons for buying such a unit, but let it suffice to say it would have been very nice to have had an additional unit. I located the unit I wanted to purchase at a price that was competitive and reasonable, however I would have to finance this machine. I had some other bills that needed to be paid off first, and we needed a new bedroom suite, much more than we needed a computer.

Financing was not a problem; the money for the payment was not a problem. The problem was I promised Glenda (my wife) the bedroom set before I bought the computer. And I promised to pay cash and not finance the computer. The temptation was very great to buy the computer. But I needed more patience in dealing with my kids so, guess what? It was over a year later when I got the computer and I paid cash. I got along better with everyone as I became more patient.

I am convinced when James said to let patience have her perfect work, that you may be perfect and entire, wanting nothing, he was talking about becoming a complete Christian, able to give love and be an example to the younger believer.

How then should we walk in the area of long-suffering? Carefully. Not yielding to temptation. Not buckling under the trials of our faith. Walking as an example to others, and showing God's love to those around us.

As we look around us today we see an ever-increasing debt load on our country. Why? Because we must have it now! If we examine the budget of our government we discover that current trust fund money is being used to balance a budget that will allow for tax cuts or more spending or both. The end result is more debt. The trends that began in the '70's and '80's continue today to create a crushing weight of debt. Fewer and fewer people own their own homes because of first, second and third tier mortgages. Lack of patience and instant gratification continue to destroy us. We want it now and we want it all now.

We lose our Christian witness when we become so impatient that we cut people off, etc. I have seen cartoons that show the best route to avoid "road rage." Flight attendants regularly deal with "air rage." If you look at social media you can see instances of "straw rage," "political rage," and rage about just everything else. We are fast becoming a society that is in a rage about everything. That rage is from the very pits of Hell. It is the rage of satan loose in our society.

Our impatience destroys. Godly patience builds. The great cathedrals of our world were built over time with great love. Just a few years ago the last stone was laid on the National Cathedral in Washington, DC. It took over 80 years to build the building and it is incredible. We can't wait that long any more. We want it today. Faster and faster.

If anything destroys this country it will be our rush to get everything. If we are patient and work on our relationship with God, we will gain everything.

SCRIPTURE ON PATIENCE/LONGSUFFERING FOR REFLECTION

Exodus 34:6

Numbers 14:18

Numbers 24:18

Psalm 86:15

Ecclesiastes 7:81

Nahum 1:3

Luke 8:15

Romans 2:3 – 4

Romans 2:6-7

Romans 8:24-25

1 Corinthians 9:25

1 Corinthians 13:4

2 Corinthians 1:6

2 Corinthians 12:12

Ephesians 4:1 – 3

Colossians 1:9 – 12

Colossians 3:12 – 13

1 Thessalonians 5:14

1 Timothy 1:16

2 Timothy 4:1 – 2

Hebrews 6:11 – 12

James 5:7 – 8

1 Peter 2:20

1 Peter 3:9

2 Peter 1:5 – 7

CHAPTER SIX

THE FRUIT OF KINDNESS

Jesus replied and said, "A man was going down from Jerusalem to Jericho, and fell among robbers, and they stripped him and beat him, and went away leaving him half dead. "And by chance a priest was going down on that road, and when he saw him, he passed by on the other side. "Likewise, a Levite also, when he came to the place and saw him, passed by on the other side. "But a Samaritan, who was on a journey, came upon him; and when he saw him, he felt compassion, and came to him and bandaged up his wounds, pouring oil and wine on them; and he put him on his own beast, and brought him to an inn and took care of him. "On the next day he took out two denarii and gave them to the innkeeper and said, 'Take care of him; and whatever more you spend, when I return I will repay you.' "Which of these three do you think proved to be a neighbor to the man who fell into the robbers' hands?" And he said, "The one who showed mercy toward him." Then Jesus said to him, "Go and do the same."   Luke 10:30-37 NASB

As we move into our next fruit for discussion, we need first to define our beginning point. In the King James Version, we have the word <u>Gentleness</u>, New King James, Revised Standard Version, Today's English Version, New International Version, and the New American Standard all use the word <u>Kindness</u> for this next fruit. My own research indicates this is the correct usage of the Greek. When we look at the fruit of Meekness we will see the word gentleness used properly.

When the church talks about kindness there is one passage of Scripture that is almost always discussed, Luke 10:30-37. It is the text of the "Good Samaritan" story. Church people have all heard the story and told the story and read the story, and yet we do not live the story in our society. We are gripped with fear as we travel life's journey because we are all too familiar with the faked injury that leads to harm. We live in a world that has gone "mad" and will riot at the drop of a hat, or good and bad news events. We are increasingly aware of the danger of getting involved in another person's tragedy.

I read recently of a man who one day was stranded and for an hour or so, no one stopped to help him with his broken-down vehicle, finally a man of Hispanic decent, speaking only Spanish stopped to help. That person decided to never pass someone in need along the highway. He also tells of the fear that gripped his heart and the fact that he soon was not helping because of that fear. He decided that if he helped just ten people that would be enough. He has since helped many more than the original ten, and has told his story to all that he helped, asking them to help just ten other people.

It takes very little thought to realize where such a program of helping others could and would take us as a nation. We cannot redefine the Scripture so we must learn to live in light of the Scripture, on a daily basis, in the midst of the insanity. We shall try to answer this dilemma as we proceed through our discussion of kindness.

KINDNESS AS AN ATTRIBUTE

Let us turn our attention to God and define first that He is the God of kindness, and as we do so we shall see linked again to this wonderful God that we serve, the relationship of love to kindness.

> *"They refused to listen, and did not remember Your wondrous deeds which You had performed among them; So, they became stubborn and appointed a leader to return to their slavery in Egypt. But You are a God of forgiveness, <u>Gracious and compassionate, Slow to anger and abounding in lovingkindness; And You did not forsake them</u>.*
>
> Nehemiah 9:17 NASB

I have underlined the second half of this verse so you will pay close attention to the words. Israel has sinned against God and had been called to a day of national repentance. In writing the text, the author Nehemiah, notes that they did not remember the wondrous deeds of God, but in the last part we find God did not forget the people, He called them to be His own. God is gracious, compassionate, slow to anger, and abounding in loving kindness. What a God!

You will immediately see that we are serve a God of great kindness as we read this Scripture, it is also important to notice the linking of slow to anger with kindness. We serve a longsuffering, kindness showing God. God withheld the punishment in His mercy to show His kindness. Some will argue that God is vengeful, and you can read Scripture in that manner. But, if you will examine the whole of Scripture, God's wrath is only poured out when God's Law and Holiness is violated. When God's Law is obeyed, God's blessing follow.

Webster defines kindness this way:
1. A kind deed, favor
2. a. The quality or state of being kind.
   b. Affection.

Affection speaks of the love relationship here between kindness and love. We need to add a definition here for kindness. When we use this word, it is not in the relationship usage but in the action usage of the word. Webster goes on with his definition thus:

1. Affectionate, loving.
2. a. Of a sympathetic nature: disposed to be helpful and solicitous.
   b. Of a forbearing nature gentle.
   c. Arising from or characterized by sympathy or forbearance.
3. Of a kind to give pleasure or relief; agreeable.

There are many Scriptures to declare God's kindness to man. Here is a sampling of passages on kindness as it applies to our lives.

But the LORD was with Joseph and extended kindness to him, and gave him favor in the sight of the chief jailer. Genesis 39:21 NASB

Let the righteous smite me in kindness and reprove me; It is oil upon the head; Do not let my head refuse it... Psalm 141:5 NASB

Do not let kindness and truth leave you; Bind them around your neck, Write them on the tablet of your heart. Proverbs 3:3 NASB

Will they not go astray who devise evil? But kindness and truth will be to those who devise good. Proverbs 14:22 NASB

What is desirable in a man is his kindness... Proverbs 19:22 NASB

She opens her mouth in wisdom, And the teaching of kindness is on her tongue.   Proverbs 31:26 NASB

Therefore, return to your God, Observe kindness and justice...   Hosea 12:6 NASB

in purity, in knowledge, in patience, in kindness, in the Holy Spirit, in genuine love,
                2 Corinthians 6:6 NASB

so that in the ages to come He might show the surpassing riches of His grace in kindness toward us in Christ Jesus.   Ephesians 2:7 NASB

But when the kindness of God our Savior and His love for mankind appeared,   Titus 3:4 NASB

...if you have tasted the kindness of the Lord.
                1 Peter 2:3 NASB

and in your godliness, brotherly kindness, and in your brotherly kindness, love.   2 Peter 1:7 NASB

KINDNESS AS EMOTION

In the second part of Webster's definition regarding kindness it states kindness is affectionate, loving. To try to operate as a kind person without some emotional attachment to the act of kindness is in my opinion impossible. Ask yourself about the last time you acted in pure kindness. Why did you do it? I am sure there are several good answers such as it just seemed the right thing to do, I wanted to help, and they really needed some kindness that day. If we collaborated we could fill several pages I am sure. But, let me ask you again, why did you do it? This time think about what if you had not done the act of kindness?

Sometimes we simply know to do the right thing. I remember hearing a preacher, and I even know his name 35 plus years later, talk about how he had done a simple random act of kindness that week. His message was on kindness and he had had an experience that found its way into the message. It was a simple act that the person for whom it was done will never know it was done for them. Here is what he did, he saw that a neighbor's storm door was swinging in the wind. It was a windy day and he knew the neighbor had left for the day and by the time they would return home the door would likely be torn off its hinges. The preacher stopped his car, walked up to the door and closed it securely. Not much of a big deal, until you consider the cost of a new door. As I am writing this in 2020 that type of door would cost $300 to $500 dollars installed. A simple act with big outcomes.

Why should the preacher stop and take care of a simple door? Where is the emotion in that you ask? I get emotional over $500 that I did not need to spend. But maybe that is not the emotion we need.

The emotion comes when we realize that except for the grace of God that is us. It might be the kid who needs new shoes, or the child trying to put air into the tire of their bicycle at the neighborhood gas station and does not have a good idea on how to do it just yet. Could it be that the heart strings get touched as we look around and see that we could help, if we wanted? The story of Scrooge has captivated Christmas for most of my life. You cannot watch a Christmas movie that does not have a Scrooge.

Because so many hate Scrooge we all cheer when the Scrooge character finally gets it and does something kind.

There is a heart there after all, and we get our holiday fix of good feelings. Except for God's grace in our lives we are Scrooge. We become uncaring, unfeeling, and unconcerned with those around us. Activate the emotion of compassion and we become caring, feeling, concerned people who will act in kindness to those around us.

Compassion for people is only found in the Cross of Jesus Christ. I have had people tell me otherwise, but life has taught me when someone has to tell you they are compassionate toward people, they are in it for themselves. In your life as a Christian, seek compassion for people and do acts of kindness. True acts of kindness seek no reward.

THE ANTITHESIS OF KINDNESS

Thinking about the antithesis of kindness evokes several possibilities. Certainly, the bully generally lacks kindness, the apathetic lacks kindness, or just the plain old mean person who is never kind. I could not argue with even one of these descriptions as being an opposite of kindness. But I also think there might just be another component that is at the root of all of these. The critical spirit.

For the last one hundred years we have talked about the "Gay Nineties" with something of awe and affection. The time was 1890 and the spirit of the country was joyous. Thirty years later we would have the 'Roaring 20's". We have lived through "Raging Nineties". Raging because it brought about "Road Rage," "Air Rage," "School Rage," and "Postal Worker Rage."

I stood on line for almost six hours one night to get re-ticketed for my return home to Kansas City after bad weather distorted the schedule of a major airline. The airline was very inefficient and the customers were getting angry about the increasingly long wait. One person remarked that the only thing missing was a few AK-47 guns and we would have thought it was the Post Office.

The point of the comment was that the rage factor was climbing among the customers. While it does not take a "full blown" rage to be the opposite of kindness, it is the actions we take in response to someone's treatment of us that indicates how well we are doing with the issue of kindness. Some might interpret my comments to be that we are never angry enough to say or do something about wrong situations. If they do they are mistaken.

In the mist of the horrendous wait, I personally called aside a customer service representative and loudly complained about the fact that children and senior citizens were not being treated properly and that they were not doing their job properly by insuring that line crashers were dealt with properly. I was not unkind in my comments, and my fellow passengers cheered loudly after I had finished. I did not threaten, abuse or demand, I simply pointed out the problems in a very straight forward manner.

Kindness does not rage, bully or threaten. Kindness is straight forward, honest, and clear. Kindness can be evident even in difficult situations. Kindness does no harm to either the physical person or the emotional person. Kindness makes the point in such a way that a child is not frightened, but an adult gets the message without fear of physical violence. Rage too, gets the message across and children are frightened and adults are fearful or ready to fight.

My concern for this time in history is that we will learn to handle our rages as we are pushed and pushed and pushed toward exhaustion and burnout. We are living in an instant gratification society, we make fewer provisions necessary for the physical person. If we had been standing in line a hundred years ago there would have been provision made for the comfort of the elderly.

We have let the pressures of this world push us and push us until we have no compassion for people. We are looking out for "number one" and number one only. We care only for ourselves, and we feel we have such a right to having our own wants met that no one else matters. Kindness says my wants are no more important than yours; and I will help you with yours, without anger or malice.

Kindness vs. Rage. This is the battle we are faced with. The Scripture says

> _Be kind to one another_, tender-hearted, forgiving each other, just as God in Christ also has forgiven you.   Ephesians 4:32 NASB
>   (underline mine)

Criticism can and does bully people. Criticism is often because of a sense of superiority, it is apathetic to the feelings that their behavior evokes in another, and as a result they are not seen as kind people at all.

Let me give you an example, from a recent encounter with a person. In the time we were together maybe six sentences were spoken by the other person. Four of those sentences were critical of something I said or did. The encounter lasted less than ten minutes. It has been several days now and I still feel the sting of that event. Why does it bother me? One, I care about the person.

Two, I don't feel I did anything so horrible that it needed the verbal attacks I received.

While the aforementioned example is mine and mine alone to deal with, it is representative of what happens in many lives today. Rather than taking a constructive and kind route, we take a critical and condemning route. Notice what Jesus said during the Sermon on the Mount:

> "Do not judge so that you will not be judged. "For in the way you judge, you will be judged; and by your standard of measure, it will be measured to you. "Why do you look at the speck that is in your brother's eye, but do not notice the log that is in your own eye? "Or how can you say to your brother, 'Let me take the speck out of your eye,' and behold, the log is in your own eye? "You hypocrite, first take the log out of your own eye, and then you will see clearly to take the speck out of your brother's eye.
>
> Matthew 7:1-5 NASB

When we are critical of others we play into the enemy's hand. Before we move forward, we need to ask it is ever okay to judge a situation? The answer is yes. These judgements need to take place in light of what God's word states clearly, and then if necessary discussed with the offending person. Keeping in mind two very crucial things, first the Biblical plan for fixing a problem between Christians found in Matthew 18:15 and this passage from Ephesians:

> As a result, we are no longer to be children, tossed here and there by waves and carried about by every wind of doctrine, by the trickery of men, by craftiness in deceitful scheming; but speaking the truth in love, we are to grow up in all aspects into Him who is the head, even Christ, from whom the

whole body, being fitted and held together by what
every joint supplies, according to the proper working
of each individual part, causes the growth of the
body for the building up of itself in love.
                                    Ephesians 4:14-16 NASB

Notice my underline. Speaking the truth in love. Not
flippant, not nastily, not arrogantly, not demeaning the
other person, but spoken lovingly. Anything else and we
play into the hands of the destroyer of relationships and
family.

THE KINDNESS LOVE CONNECTION

We cannot separate out kindness without acknowledging
the love relationship again and again. We most often find
God linked with kindness when we see Him linked with
Love such as in the following verses:

For Your lovingkindness is before my eyes, And I
have walked in Your truth.   Psalms 26:3 NASB

How precious is Your lovingkindness, O God! And
the children of men take refuge in the shadow of
Your wings.   Psalms 36:7 NASB

Because Your lovingkindness is better than life, my
lips will praise You.   Psalms 63:3 NASB

Answer me, O LORD, for Your lovingkindness is
good; According to the greatness of Your
compassion, turn to me,   Psalms 69:16 NASB

I shall make mention of the lovingkindnesses of the
LORD, the praises of the LORD, according to all
that the LORD has granted us, And the great

goodness toward the house of Israel, Which He has granted them according to His compassion and according to the abundance of His lovingkindnesses.
Isaiah 63:7 NASB

I could sight verse after verse after verse that would link these two words together and describe the kindness of the LORD God whom we serve. But it is not necessary to look that hard to see such a readily visible trait of our God. It is important to realize that God is a whole person. We often fragment Him in our teaching and thinking. We see Him only as a judge, or an angry potentate (judge) handing out justice upon sinners, or as the King of Glory worthy of our worship, and sometimes as a Spirit enveloping the earth in His omnipresence. We see Him as all-knowing and we fail to recognize that He is a fully developed being with fully developed attributes of personality. It is from this fully developed person, this wonderful God of creation that we receive the instructions of how we should live. Kindness is one of those wonderful parts of our lives we are to develop to its fullest potential. We can define kindness, we can see kindness but how do we implement kindness?

We must recognize that kindness comes from a loving heart. There are many ways in which to live this life, some will choose to be hermits. I read an article recently on the life of Greta Garbo, a famous actress of the 30's and 40's and how she lived much of the last 30 years of her life as a hermit in the city of New York, only going out with a select few people and they not knowing even her phone number. She would call them, but they could not call her.

We could live like that, or we can live on the other extreme of this wonderful dilemma of life. We could live like a person I heard call into a talk show who was describing a psychological disorder called "extreme compassion disorder". It seems she could not stand for anyone to suffer and that she would go out of the way to help and then do so even if it cost some of her own money. At times her family would have to wait to have some item or another so that they could help the person in need. To me it sounded like a person who had been struck with the compassion of Christ, but to the talk show audience it was a sad thing for one to be so innocent and giving. If perhaps this is an extreme to be avoided, then how should we live? We must live according to the Holy Scriptures, our Bibles.

Paul's letter to Titus chapter 3 will start us on the track we wish to take:

> *Remind them to be subject to rulers, to authorities, to be obedient, to be ready for every good deed, to malign no one, to be peaceable, gentle, showing every consideration for all men. For we also once were foolish ourselves, disobedient, deceived, enslaved to various lusts and pleasures, spending our life in malice and envy, hateful, hating one another.* <u>*But when the kindness of God our Savior and His love for mankind appeared, He saved us, not on the basis of deeds which we have done in righteousness, but according to His mercy,*</u> *by the washing of regeneration and renewing by the Holy Spirit, whom He poured out upon us richly through Jesus Christ our Savior, so that being justified by His grace we would be made heirs according to the hope of eternal life. (my underline)*Titus 3:1-7 NASB

Notice if you will the areas of life that Paul addresses here in this portion of Scripture:

1. Subject to those in authority;
2. Obey those in authority;
3. Ready to do every good deed;
4. Speak evil of no man;
5. Not brawlers;
6. Gentle showing consideration for all people.

After listing these characteristics Paul brings us to our discussion of the "Kindness of God", it is unto our redemption. Again, as with longsuffering we are the book that is read, our kindness reflects the kindness of God. A glass of water given in the name of the Lord is sometimes enough to inspire an individual to seek God's favor.

> *"For whoever gives you a cup of water to drink because of your name as followers of Christ, truly I say to you, he will not lose his reward.*
> Mark 9:41 NASB

When we talk about kindness it is easy to quickly turn our thoughts to the poor of our society. We are often moved by compassion for those who are in need of material items, and it is easy to soothe our conscience by assisting in some way the poor. Many verses of Scripture concerning the righteous and the poor describe the wonderful blessings of being of assistance to the poor. An excellent example is from the Proverbs:

> *He who oppresses the poor taunts his Maker, but he who is gracious to the needy honors Him.*
> Proverbs 14:31 NASB

We, of the community of Christ, the body, the church of our Lord and Savior, must come to the realization that our kindness must stretch to the lowest to the highest person in the land. I often hear people degrading the person for whom they work, many is the time I have heard a pastor ripped over the coals by a parishioner (a few times I was that pastor). I wouldn't take that person to a "worm wrestle" was a favorite saying of mine a few years back, when I was a youth pastor. And even though I would never have said it to the person in question, to their face, the Scriptures teach that as a man thinks in his heart so is he. A simple rule to apply is "Don't say anything about a person you would not say about them if they were in the same room you are in and within hearing distance."

Proclaiming such simple things as "I wouldn't give that person the time of day", tells everyone around you that the next time you say "I'll be praying for them" or "you," you really don't mean it because you are not even kind enough to give them the "time of day". Kindness must come from every part of our being, our actions our deeds, our words, even our thoughts.

Our thoughts sometimes, even though we are the only one privy to them, are often displayed across the lines of our face so loudly no one had to read them to know what we are thinking. Our all and everything must bear the resemblance of Christ. Otherwise we serve with less than our whole heart, and we have not the love of Christ within us. We must be loving those around us, with His Love.

Lovingkindness Found 120 Times in Psalms (NASB)

Psalm 6:4	*Psalm 17:7*
Psalm 13:5	*Psalm 18:50*

Psalm 21:7

Psalm 23:6

Psalm 25:7

Psalm 25:10

Psalm 26:3

Psalm 31:7

Psalm 31:16

Psalm 31:21

Psalm 32:10

Psalm 33:5

Psalm 33:18

Psalm 33:22

Psalm 36:5

Psalm 36:7

Psalm 36:10

Psalm 40:10

Psalm 40:11

Psalm 42:8

Psalm 44:26

Psalm 48:9

Psalm 51:1

Psalm 52:1

Psalm 52:8

Psalm 57:3

Psalm 57:10

Psalm 59:10

Psalm 59:16

Psalm 59:17

Psalm 61:7

Psalm 62:12

Psalm 63:3

Psalm 66:20

Psalm 69:13

Psalm 69:16

Psalm 77:8

Psalm 85:7

Psalm 85:10

Psalm 86:5

Psalm 86:13

Psalm 86:15

Psalm 88:11

Psalm 89:1

Psalm 89:2

Psalm 89:14

Psalm 89:24

Psalm 89:28

Psalm 89:33

Psalm 90:14

Psalm 92:2

Psalm 94:18

Psalm 98:3

Psalm 100:5

Psalm 101:1

Psalm 103:4

Psalm 103:8

Psalm 103:11

Psalm 103:17

Psalm 106:1

Psalm 106:45

Psalm 107:1

Psalm 107:8

Psalm 107:15

Psalm 107:21

Psalm 107:31

Psalm 108:4

Psalm 109:12

Psalm 109:16

Psalm 109:21

Psalm 109:26

Psalm 115:1

Psalm 117:2

Psalm 118:1

Psalm 118:2

Psalm 118:3

Psalm 118:4

Psalm 118:29

Psalm 119:64

Psalm 119:76

Psalm 119:88

Psalm 119:124

Psalm 119:149

Psalm 119:159

Psalm 130:7

Psalm 136:1

Psalm 136:2

Psalm 136:3

Psalm 136:4

Psalm 136:5

Psalm 136:6

Psalm 136:7

Psalm 136:8

Psalm 136:9

Psalm 136:10   Psalm 136:22

Psalm 136:11   Psalm 136:23

Psalm 136:12   Psalm 136:24

Psalm 136:13   Psalm 136:25

Psalm 136:14   Psalm 136:26

Psalm 136:15   Psalm 138:2

Psalm 136:16   Psalm 138:8

Psalm 136:17   Psalm 143:8

Psalm 136:18   Psalm 143:12

Psalm 136:19   Psalm 144:2

Psalm 136:20   Psalm 145:8

Psalm 136:21   Psalm 147:11

CHAPTER SEVEN

THE FRUIT OF GOODNESS

As He was setting out on a journey, a man ran up to Him and knelt before Him, and asked Him, "Good Teacher, what shall I do to inherit eternal life?" And Jesus said to him, "Why do you call Me good? No one is good except God alone. Mark 10:17-18 NASB

As we begin the discussion for our next fruit we realize that there is only one truly good person and we have the privilege of knowing the Father, God Almighty who is the only true good being.

The story surrounding this passage is the story of the rich young ruler, the point we are interested in is the summation of Jesus concerning Our Father, God. There is none good, says Christ, and we must concur. He was taking about humanity. No matter how good we want to be there is none that is good! The young ruler calls Jesus good, however the Greek man infers good as by achievement, when Jesus speaks it is about good as character. This distinction is important. We can all do good deeds, but that does not necessarily make us good. Take the corrupt business man who does "good" to get "good will" while mistreating employees and business partners.

The character of God is goodness. The supreme goodness of God gives us a goal to be achieved, but for some it is a goal that if they cannot reach so they settle for doing all they can to oppose it. There is a trend I have seen in the past few years to take the attitude "I don't want to be good, none of my friends are good people. Therefore, why would I want to be a good person or even a Christian?

None my friends will be going to heaven." Attitudes of "they treated me bad so I will destroy them" are contrary to the life we are called to live as Christians.

As I write today I am in sorrow as another city is undergoing violence caused by the death of a man at the hands of another. Men who knew each other, one white one black has caused rioting in the streets. Something bad happened and people who had no connection to the event are destroying a city for the sake of destruction, seeking to get even for any and every bad thing that has ever happened to them both real and imagined.

Why? They lack any sense of goodness. Jesus was right when he said there "no one is good." There is much to discuss on this in Scripture. Let us begin.

GOODNESS AS AN ATTRIBUTE

Examine the following Scriptural basis for calling God good.

> *O give thanks to the LORD, for He is good; For His lovingkindness is everlasting.*
> 1 Chronicles 16:34 NASB

> *...bowed down on the pavement with their faces to the ground, and they worshiped and gave praise to the LORD, saying, "Truly He is good, truly His lovingkindness is everlasting."*
> 2 Chronicles 7:3b NASB

> *They sang, praising and giving thanks to the LORD, saying, "For He is good, for His lovingkindness is upon Israel forever." And all the people shouted with a great shout when they praised*

the LORD because the foundation of the house of the LORD was laid.

Ezra 3:11 NASB

Good and upright is the LORD; Therefore, He instructs sinners in the way. Psalms 25:8 NASB

O taste and see that the LORD is good; How blessed is the man who takes refuge in Him!

Psalms 34:8 NASB

For the LORD is good; His lovingkindness is everlasting And His faithfulness to all generations.

Psalms 100:5 NASB

Praise the LORD! Oh, give thanks to the LORD, for He is good; For His lovingkindness is everlasting.

Psalms 106:1 NASB

Oh, give thanks to the LORD, for He is good, For His lovingkindness is everlasting. Psalms 107:1 NASB

We see over and over again that God is the good God we know Him to be and have grown to trust Him as, we must also note that Jesus shares this attribute with the Father and declares of Himself in John 10:11:

"I am the good shepherd, and I know My own and My own know Me, John 10:14 NASB.

When we think of goodness there is just no other example than that of God. Among men there is none that is entirely good. We strive for goodness but then without thinking we do something that upsets someone around us and we are to them no longer "good."

I served on a board recently, and had the responsibility of confronting a member governed by that board. Before the needed confrontation we were friends. Now the person does not speak to me. I miss the friendship and even though I am no longer on that board the relationship is lost. I am no longer "good" to that person.

We have in this life no example of good that is lasting and meaningful. I had the opportunity to watch a special where the commentator was interviewing a man whom I thought was a good man and a devout man trying to do some good with his life and influence, and yet as the interview progressed I discovered that this man was an anarchist, self-important, un-accepting of others, and concerned only with his personal goals even if that meant pain or hurt for others.

Again, we are taken back to the verse we started with,

"No one is good except God alone." Mark 10: 18 NASB

Recognize with me that goodness is another illusive fruit and yet it is something that we must strive for in our Christian life much like all the other Fruits of the Spirit.

We may question why we should strive for any of the fruit if we cannot obtain them in their totality, so let us liken them to the runner, and borrow from the illustration of Paul when he spoke of the runners running but only one wins first prize (I Cor. 9:24). The winner of any race does not always set a record, and every time a race is run of specific distance, that distance's record is in jeopardy of being broken. For the runner and the record every race is a challenge. The runner runs not only to win over his challengers but to beat the record.

As Christians, we run not only to be better than we were but to ascribe to a better order, to be more like Christ, to draw nearer to perfection. We recognize then that goodness toward our fellowman comes out of the love that we have for God, and the love that He gives us for the world around us, out of the compassion of Christ within us.

GOODNESS AS AN EMOTION

Goodness is not really an emotion. It is a chosen response to an emotion. The emotion of caring. Not all professional psychologists recognize care as an emotion. Please don't tell them they are wrong. The emotion of care causes us to make certain we "take care of" the weaker members of our families. Because we care we feed them, change those diapers, and make sure they have medical assistance. From this emotion of care springs forth the desire to do "good." When the emotion of care is stifled we see evil rather than good.

If we do not choose goodness then evil will abound. If you have ever said this world is going downhill, or thought it based on the lack of caring and evilness in our society, you are not wrong. It is a problem that has been around for centuries. It does seem to be spiraling faster downhill these days and I submit to you that in part the problem is we are a very narcissistic[1] society. We may not all suffer from the condition of narcissism, but we behave as though we have it.

How many times have we heard "it is all about me?" or seen behavior that represents itself in apathy toward the needs of others with a sense of entitlement and unable to handle criticism. These are the symptoms of narcissism and they are rampant among the current generation.

When narcissism prevails, goodness suffers. When our emotions are tied to the values of narcissism we do not consider doing good unto others. In days gone past every child learned the golden rule, it is from Matthew

> *"In everything, therefore, treat people the same way you want them to treat you, for this is the Law and the Prophets.* Matthew 7:12 NASB

Today the narcissistic culture has changed the rule to say, "he who has the gold rules." With this attitude goodness is a fading part of our society at large. Yes, there are good things that good people do every day, but there is a need for all people to do good things every day. When we get our emotional "care" in proper perspective our goodness can grow led by God's Holy Spirit, for only God is Good.

THE ANTITHESIS OF GOODNESS

As I write it almost seems that I could skip this section totally. Why? The very essence of the opposite to goodness is evil. Much has been written debating the existence of evil, claiming evil behavior is bad parenting, bad social experiences and at one time in history, bad genetics. If your parent was bad you were guilty by association, you had "bad blood."

I do not subscribe to bad blood, or bad social influences. I will accept bad parenting to a point, but there is a time in all of our lives we decide about good and evil in our own life. If you are reading this book you most likely have decided to pursue goodness over evil, to pursue Christ over the enemy. I applaud you for that decision, and you no doubt are aware of how hard it can be to remain committed to the decision. I want to spend a few inches of this book reviewing three pertinent Scripture about over coming evil. Here they are:

Let love be without hypocrisy. Abhor what is evil; cling to what is good. Romans 12:9 NASB

Do not be overcome by evil, but overcome evil with good. Romans 12:21 NASB

Therefore, take up the full armor of God, so that you will be able to resist in the evil day, and having done everything, to stand firm.
Ephesians 6:13 NASB

Love without hypocrisy. On the surface it seems that love would be without hypocrisy or it isn't really love. Here in lies the problem. People will give "love" to get most anything.

I love to tell jokes, and I tell lots of them. Sometimes I bomb, but I do pretty well at is. There is a joke that has come to mean a lot to me in recent weeks for reasons I don't need to discuss, it goes like this. When you are an infant they get you diapers that are named things like pampers, huggies, luvs and such. We do that because we pamper babies, give them lots of hugs, and love (luv) on them lots and lots. As a baby you can do no wrong, but when you get to the other end of life and you have to wear "diapers" again because of incontinence you get "depends" for a diaper. The reason they are called depends is the only ones who will help you at this point in life are depending on being in the will.

The essence of what I want you to understand is if people will give "love" only if their name is in the will it is love with hypocrisy. Paul warns against it in this passage from

Romans, and he adds Abhor[2] that which is evil. Abhor is such a powerful word. It means to regard with disgust and hatred; to regard with extreme repugnance: to feel hatred or loathing for.

Abhor is about as far from liking something as you can get. Think of a food you despise. Mine is rutabaga. How much will you do to get out of eating that food right now? That is abhor.

You will never win the battle with evil if you fight the way evil fights. You are way too young to be as experienced as the master craftsman of evil, the enemy of your soul. You can say "but it is just another person I am battling with," but the battle is not of this world. The battle is not even yours. The battle the Bible says is the Lord's.

> *"and he said, "Listen, all Judah and the inhabitants of Jerusalem and King Jehoshaphat: thus, says the LORD to you, 'Do not fear or be dismayed because of this great multitude, for the battle is not yours but God's."* 2 Chronicles 20:15 NASB

If you have never undertaken a study of the armor of God from Ephesians (6:10-20) let me encourage you to do so when you finish this book. Personally, I think the imagery is some of the best. The Sword of the Lord, which is the Word of God, the Helmet of Salvation, how critical for our thinking and understanding of God. With all imagery presented in this passage the final word is to STAND. I can write all day, and pull in more and more Scripture about dealing with evil, but if you don't take a stand against evil and then stand firm in your choice you will never develop the fruit of Goodness in your life.

GOODNESS AND THE LOVE CONNECTION

(Love) ...does not act unbecomingly; it does not seek its own, is not provoked, does not take into account a wrong suffered,   1 Corinthians 13:5 NASB

Notice if you will the text above, love does not do those things that are contrary to goodness. Love rejects thoughts that are about evil.

There is a phrase "I don't get mad I get even." This phrase is perhaps the embodiment of all that goodness and love are not. As we examine the mind set behind this statement we observe that to even declare that we will get even is to begin to plot and prepare to do some deed that is an unworthy response to that which has angered us. Unworthy as it does not embody what it is to be a Christian, and it shows a lack of goodness

It is the beginning of thinking about evil. I recognize that we often use such a phrase as a comic response to another's plight. However, if the comment is meant in any way other than jest it deviates from the Scriptural pattern of turning the other cheek.[3] If we walk the path of vengeance we have walked into a place where goodness struggles to live.

Saying I don't "get mad but even" can have its place as a tension breaker. Goodness, however. Is the art and act of giving and returning the Love of God in spite of a problem.

If you want to be a successful witness to those whom are your enemies, then begin to show them kindness with goodness. A kind act does not have to come from a goodness motivation. Acts of kindness can be self-serving, but kindness out of goodness is done without thought of gain or personal advancements. It is pure in its motivation.

> *Never pay back evil for evil to anyone. Respect what is right in the sight of all men. If possible, so far as it depends on you, be at peace with all men. Never take your own revenge, beloved, but leave room for the wrath of God, for it is written, "VENGEANCE IS MINE, I WILL REPAY," says the Lord. "BUT IF YOUR ENEMY IS HUNGRY, FEED HIM, AND IF HE IS THIRSTY, GIVE HIM A DRINK; FOR IN SO DOING YOU WILL HEAP BURNING COALS ON HIS HEAD." Do not be overcome by evil, but overcome evil with good.*
> *Romans 12:17-21 NASB*

David has been described as a man after God's own heart; he underwent some very severe trials before coming to the throne after Saul's death. Saul tried 21 times to kill David, each one unsuccessful, but after the twentieth try David and Saul meet, and they have an exchange of words. Saul in closing the encounter says to David:

> *He said to David, "You are more righteous than I; for you have dealt well with me, while I have dealt wickedly with you.* 1 Samuel 24:17 NASB

David was a good, kind, and honorable man the majority of the days of his life. What I truly love about David is he was human and made a few mistakes along the way, yet Scripture[4] records that he was a man after God's own heart.

I Corinthians 13:6 says that [Love].... *does not rejoice in unrighteousness, but rejoices with the truth.* The King James uses a word that has pretty much fallen by the wayside in the church world for unrighteousness here, that word is iniquity. Iniquity is sin. The best definition of iniquity I have ever read was that it is the sin that we know about and have asked forgiveness for, yet we continue to do it.

Some examples of iniquity that bring destruction are gluttony, sexual sins, lying, exaggerating, addictions such as drugs and alcohol. There are some who will dismiss my contention that drugs and alcohol are sins of addiction. Let us save that debate for another day. With any iniquity, forgiveness from God can set you free. Iniquity is evil, manifesting in our lives to destroy our relationship with the Father. If repetitive sin is not what iniquity is, then we must still concede it is sin and it is still evil in God's sight. It is evil manifesting itself in our lives and can be cured by forgiveness from God above.

Love finds no joy in evil. Love cannot abide the evil, it is to be hated. Amos tell us

> *Seek good and not evil, that you may live; And thus, may the LORD God of hosts be with you, just as you have said! Hate evil, love good, and establish justice in the gate!* Amos 5:14-15a NASB

Paul said it this way in Romans

> *"Let love be without hypocrisy. Abhor what is evil; cling to what is good."* Romans 12:9 NASB

Let love be without false pretense, let it be genuine.

Paul continues on in this passage pointing out how we should behave. We are to be affectionate, give preference to others, not lagging in diligence and fervent in spirit. He also comments on staying hopeful, steadfast in prayer, giving, and being hospitable, blessing those who persecute and being same minded one to another. We could spend hours dissecting this passage as it contains incredible amounts of wisdom on how to be "good" to our fellow Christians.

Love the sinner but hate the evil within them. Let it be love that is real, not put on because it is required of you. If a Missionary or Pastor is in charge of a flock, and does not have a love for their people that transcends all of their faults and shortcomings, they will know it, and be offended by it. Love has to be pure and the evil must be hated. I have always liked the choice of words here, abhor is such a strong word, and cleave has connotations on hanging on when all is falling around you. Abhor the evil, cleave to the good, and the goodness that is our responsibility to develop as a fruit will grow within.

John puts all of this into perspective

> *Beloved, do not imitate what is evil, but what is good. The one who does good is of God; the one who does evil has not seen God.*　　3 John 11 NASB

Hebrews puts it this way:

> *and let us consider how to stimulate one another to love and good deeds,*　　Hebrew 10:24 NASB

And in conclusion I Peter states:

> *For, "the one who desires life, to love and see good days, must keep his tongue from evil and his lips from speaking deceit. "he must turn away from evil and do good; he must seek peace and pursue it. "for the eyes of the lord are toward the righteous, and his ears attend to their prayer, but the face of the lord is against those who do evil."* I Peter 3:10 -12 NASB

SCRIPTURE ON GOODNESS FOR REFLECTION

1 Chronicles 16:34	*Psalms 107:1*
2 Chronicles 7:3b	*Amos 5:14-15a*
2 Chronicles 20:15	*Matthew 7:12*
Ezra 3:11	*John 10:11*
Psalms 25:8	*John 10:14*
Psalms 34:8	*Romans 12:9, 17 – 21*
Psalms 100:5	*1 Corinthians 13:5*
Psalms 106:1	*3 John 11*

CHAPTER EIGHT

THE FRUIT OF FAITH(FULNESS)

FAITHFULNESS AS AN ATTRIBUTE

One of the most difficult areas of teaching from the Scriptures comes from the work of translating the Greek or Hebrew into the English language without losing the sense of what the original manuscripts were saying. There have been many "holy wars" over the validity of a new translation, and whether or not it accurately renders the essence of the original text. One of the best examples is the Greek word πστίδς (pistis). We can find at least eight different applications of this word in the UBS Greek English Dictionary of the New Testament.[1] They include:

1. Faithful.
2. Trustworthy.
3. Reliable.
4. Believing, Believer, Christian.
5. Sure.
6. True.
7. Unfailing.
8. Sure promises, or blessings.

This simple word pistis, means in its simplest form faith, but is often rendered differently because of the context. Many modern translations label this fruit as faithfulness. We shall look at this word in light of faith and faithfulness.

As we begin we must note the following for the sake of clarity in the text of our work:

    a. Vincent's[2] word study renders our word pistis – Trustfulness.

b. The Expositors Bible Commentary[3] (NIV[4]) says it is both faith and faithfulness here.

c. Expositors Greek New Testament[5] in the footnotes says "not saving faith, but good faith in dealing with men and due regard to their just claims.

d. Jaimison, Faucett, and Brown[6] commentary says faith in the widest sense toward God and Man.

e. The Complete Biblical Library[7] translates it Faith, but notes it could be faithfulness, especially as it relates to one's relationship with others.

f. Greek English Lexicon of the New Testament based on Semantic Domains[8] by Louw and Nida says this about pistis, "to believe to the extent of complete trust and reliance - to believe in, to have confidence in, to have faith in, to trust, faith trust. "In rendering ...it would be wrong to select a term which would mean merely 'reliance' or dependency' or even 'confidence' for there should also be a significant measure of belief since real trust, confidence, and reliance can only be placed in someone who is believed to have the qualities attributed to such a person."

g. Then to add to the picture note the following from the Translators Handbook[9] series from the United Bible Societies, in the Galatians volume these words from Arichea and Nida "It is tempting to understand this in terms of man's relationship to God, but here it probably includes the elements of faithfulness, trustworthiness, honesty, trustfulness, and reliability in one's dealings with others. Faithfulness is often expressed by a verbal phrase for example, 'causes people to be trustworthy,' or 'causes people to be such that others can trust them.'

As we can quickly see there are many subtle differences in the understanding of the various authors cited and researched. To their thoughts then I add my own and I will attempt to not confuse the issue, but bring clarity to the issue. We will first deal with the word then deal with the two main points of our discussion.

Pistis is an active present tense verb. It is not a dead faith but a living faith. It is active; therefore, it is involved in the action of believing, and the action of being believable. We have no cause to disbelieve God. He is the very essence of faithfulness. Pistis is actively believing in a faithful God, and actively participating in the word in such a way as to show its faith is living and not dead.

Let me acknowledge before we move on with this study that when we discuss the fruit we have stated with confidence that each fruit to this point is an attribute of God. If we look at faith as an attribute we are unable to support the argument that each of the fruit is an attribute. God is the one who inspires faith in Himself. He does not need to have faith in Himself for He is God. However, if we understand the fruit as faithfulness, God is the epitome of Faithful. He is: (note underline)

> *If we confess our sins, He is faithful and righteous to forgive us our sins and to cleanse us from all unrighteousness.*   1 John 1:9 NASB

If we look at pistis as faithfulness then we begin to see a larger body of materials that support the premise that each of the fruit is an attribute of God.

What God brings to this discussion is His faithfulness. For all of time and for eternity we see God and we never see him wavering. James puts it this way:

Every good thing given and every perfect gift is from above, coming down from the Father of lights, with whom there is no variation or shifting shadow.
James 1:17 NASB

The CEV[10] translation renders the last half of that verse this way: "He is always the same and never makes dark shadows by changing."

For all that faith is we must recognize that it is an emotional response to the stimuli we are given. Faith, resident within man, is that which counters doubts and fears. Faith is that which allows us to say "I CAN". That is faith in ourselves. Doubt says "I can't, I don't know if this is possible." Doubt brings on fear, anxiety, and depression. Faith evokes in a man the power to say "I will", "I can", "with God's help I shall". Faith evokes an emotional drive to obtain that which we have not obtained before. Faith is an emotional response to knowledge, knowledge that says "with God I will." It may be "with God's help I will enter into the kingdom of His love," or it may be that it is "with God's help I will be faithful to those around me that need me." It may be that it is simply, "with God's help I will become all that he wants of me!"

What use is it, my brethren, if someone says he has faith but he has no works? Can that faith save him? If a brother or sister is without clothing and in need of daily food, and one of you says to them, "Go in peace, be warmed and be filled," and yet you do not give them what is necessary for their body, what use is that? Even so faith, if it has no works, is dead, being by itself. But someone may well say, "You have faith and I have works; show me your faith without the works, and I will show you my faith by my works."
James 2:14-18 NASB

James here teaches us that faith that has no future goal is dead. Faith that is not active in the presenting of the Gospel is dead. Faith that is not being faithful in presenting the practical side of the gospel, the nuts and bolts, the compassionate side, the benevolent side, the social welfare side, is dead. Works, in this context of James, is what I do and what you do that is for the benefit of another without thought of personal gain. Faith that is not faithful is dead. There may be evidence of your faith in the workings of God in your own life, but until that same faith reaches out and touches another, it is on life support or perhaps even dead. You will never reach out to another until the operation of love begins in your life in earnest. Until you care about someone else you will not know love. Until you have given of yourself in works unto the Lord you have not known a vital living faith.

Let us begin now to look at the faithfulness of God.

God is faithful, through whom you were called into fellowship with His Son, Jesus Christ our Lord.
1 Corinthians 1:9 NASB

Your lovingkindness, O LORD, extends to the heavens, your faithfulness reaches to the skies.
Psalms 36:5 NASB

I listed the New Testament Scripture first instead of the Old Testament Scripture because it is through the faithfulness of God that we have this glorious, wonderful relationship with Him. Without the faithfulness of God, we would not have experienced the salvation we know and enjoy. Our God is not a god who changes, nor is He swayed by the breezes of our thoughts, but He is faithful.

It has been said you can't count on anything. Well, you can count on the sun to rise, the moon to orbit the earth, the clouds to come and the rains to fall. You can't always tell when the clouds will come or the rain will fall, but it will happen. God has faithfully watered His earth, and provided for His creation. Man, often chooses to ignore God's programs and pay for it in his abuse of nature, but God still takes care of the earth and His creation. If we could measure faithfulness in tangible ways, David said that it would reach to the clouds.

Your lovingkindness, O LORD, extends to the heavens, your faithfulness reaches to the skies.
Psalms 36:5 NASB

I have seen a lot of clouds in my life. I have seen them from both sides, I have flown through them when they were soft and fluffy and when they were hard and turbulent. David might not have realized that God's faithfulness was above even the clouds.

I have proclaimed glad tidings of righteousness in the great congregation; Behold, I will not restrain my lips, O LORD You know, I have not hidden Your righteousness within my heart; I have spoken of Your faithfulness and Your salvation; I have not concealed Your lovingkindness and Your truth from the great congregation. Psalms 40:9, 10 NASB

David declares God's faithfulness in this passage and we have an interesting statement from David. He begins in verse nine to tell us that he has proclaimed the good news of righteousness, that he has not kept it to himself but has told the world, he then states that he has not kept truth or God's loving kindness to himself. David is telling the story of God, and all that God is, to all that will listen. He gives back faithfulness for faithfulness. Let me say that a second time; he (David) gives back faithfulness for faithfulness.

We as Christians can do nothing better than to give back, to reciprocate with, return to God faithfulness, for His faithfulness to us. We must give it back in our life style, our finances, and our compassion for others. The list is enormous, and can be overwhelming, but it comes down to a simple phrase that was popular near the turn of this last century, "What Would Jesus Do?" We are called simply to give a Godly response to each circumstance.

Do not worry if you are not perfect in doing so, you are human. However, never stop striving to do better, as you do the fruit develops within your life.

Let me direct your attention to Psalm 89. It is too much to reprint the entire chapter here, so please grab your Bible and read this chapter. I will wait for you.

If any chapter in the Bible proclaims God's faithfulness any better I have missed it. Notice if you will some of the statements made by the Psalmist:

1. (v1) God's faithfulness is to all generations.
2. (v2) God's faithfulness is established in the heavens.
3. (V5) Your faithfulness praised in the assembly of the holy ones, (saints).
4. (V8) Your faithfulness surrounds You.
5. (v24) My faithfulness and My lovingkindness will be with him.
6. (V33) I will not deal falsely in My faithfulness.
7. (v37) The witness (the moon) in the sky is faithful.

The writer of this Psalm, Ethan the Ezrahite, had a very clear understanding of the faithfulness of God. I believe we have a similar understanding but we have subjugated the faithfulness of God to science. In our efforts to understand we have denied God in much of our educational systems to the point we don't see God's faithfulness. I want you to see this faithfulness anew as you read this book. His faithfulness become the standard to reach out to in respect to our own faithfulness to God and to those around us.

A Psalm, a Song for the Sabbath Day.
It is good to give thanks to the LORD And to sing praises to Your name, O Most High; To declare Your lovingkindness in the morning And Your faithfulness by night.

Psalms 92:1-2 NASB

The Psalmist here admonishes us to consider God's faithfulness and to declare it. Perhaps you should stop for a moment and do just that. Consider, if you will, the rising of the sun, and the going down of the sun. Consider that you could eat today. Consider that you have personally seen the faithfulness of God. Robert Schuler once asked "are you better off today than you were five years ago?" Unless you have had some recent financial reversals most likely you are. And even if you are in the midst of a crisis that brings reversal, you no doubt are learning how to avoid the problems in the future that got you where you are today.

Even in the midst of troubles God's faithfulness can inspire in us faith and hope. To once again quote Roosevelt "When you reach the end of your rope, tie a knot in it and hang on." God's faithfulness gives us that hope.

Your faithfulness continues throughout all generations; You established the earth, and it stands.

Psalms 119:90 NASB

God's faithfulness endures to all generations. There is a lot of concern in our country about what type of a situation we are leaving for our kids. Social Security will be bankrupt, or so they say. The national debt will be so great that it will take everything we can earn just to pay the interest. There are doomsayers all over the place. And they may be right, but here is the one thing that I can point to and know that no matter what the outcome of all the debate is, God will still be faithful to my children and my grandchildren and great grandchildren and as many as should choose to hear the voice of God and respond to His call; the call of salvation and faithful commitment.

Does God's faithfulness remove all responsibility from me? Not in the least. If anything, I am called by our study to be more faithful as it impacts my family and my faith.

I once had a neighbor who refused to have life insurance. He had two small children. If something happened his wife would be destitute. She was concerned about it. He ignored her requests. If something happened he would be seen as unfaithful in the fiscal sense. As a Christian we have an immense responsibility to be an example of God to our world. He has shown himself faithful to us, we need to show ourselves faithful to Him and our responsibilities to our world.

Know therefore that the LORD your God is God, the faithful God who keeps covenant and steadfast love with those who love him and keep his commandments, to a thousand generations.

Deuteronomy 7:9 ESV[11]

Take a moment and just revel in this promise from God. This promise will be good for a thousand generations; as long as there are people on this earth. God will be faithful to those who keep covenant with Him. The inference in the Hebrew is that this is a promise to each one personally. As you read this Scripture the promise is to you, if you are keeping the covenant, for a thousand generations forward God will keep his part of the covenant.

FAITHFULNESS AS AN EMOTION

Thinking of faithfulness as an emotion seems at first thought to be a stretch of an idea. Remember though we have stated early in this book that the fruit are emotional responses. Faithfulness is perhaps the easiest to recognize the response part of the emotion. There are many temptations that afflict us in this life. The most prevalent is without a doubt sexual. In my life, as I am sure in yours, there have been temptations of a sexual kind. You have the responsibility to decide; do you act on the temptation or do you refrain?

Your emotions can be running wild at the thought of an encounter that would be sinful and improper, whether you are married or not the temptations are there and you have to decide. As I write this I wish I could tell you I never fell for temptations. I wish I could find, other than Jesus, that man or woman who never once gave a second thought to the temptation of sin. However, the Bible declares:

for all have sinned and fall short of the glory of God,

Romans 3:23 NASB

There has only been one who has filled the role as the sinless one. The rest of us are in the same place, Christians by the grace of God and the cleansing blood of the Lamb. Just because we are in this place, doesn't mean we can't decide about being faithful. In fact, that is what we have to do. We must reign in the emotions that run rampant as temptation calls and we choose the correct emotional response. The response is to direct our emotions toward our spouse, our family and our God.

As I have been working on this passage of the book today I was challenged by a thought that was ridiculous. I started to consider it but quickly I simply said to myself, self why would you even consider that, I want nothing between myself and my Savior. End of discussion. I chose faithfulness.

THE ANTITHESIS OF FAITHFULNESS

About the time I started this book, many years ago, a new phenomenon hit the broadcast airways of our country. The Phil Donahue and Sally Jessy Rafael shows were all the rage. People confronting other people on television. It wasn't long until we had Jerry Springer, Maury, Steve Wilkos and several others. We added Peoples Court, Divorce Court, and a dozen more court shows. To that we added Cheaters and a couple more in the same genre. By 2019 there is no civility left on the screen and the reasons people appear are so bizarre that rational people are appalled.

The one common denominator that occurs in so much of this programing is lack of faithfulness. Men and women who are cheating on the person to whom they have pledged their love. Often unmarried, because they don't want to be tied down, or rather want the freedom to be unfaithful. People appear on the court shows because they are being sued for breach of contract or some other reason that simply shows once again the lack of faithfulness.

As a society we adopted a philosophy in the 1960's that said "if it feels good, do it." The sum of the antithesis of faithfulness is found in that simple phrase. If I think it will feel good I should do it no matter the consequences. As I write this I took a break and looked at the news for this day January 30, 2019. Today, Baltimore has decided not to prosecute violators of a specific law that the District Attorney (D.A.) has decided is a waste of time. The issue here is not the crime, it is the faithlessness of the D.A. Sworn to uphold the laws of the state, the D.A. decided otherwise. As an individual they have decided not to be faithful to the pledge they have sworn.

When there is no faithfulness sin abounds.

FAITHFULNESS AND THE LOVE CONNECTION

If we say that we have fellowship with Him and yet walk in the darkness, we lie and do not practice the truth; but if we walk in the Light as He Himself is in the Light, we have fellowship with one another, and the blood of Jesus His Son cleanses us from all sin. If we say that we have no sin, we are deceiving ourselves and the truth is not in us. If we confess our sins, He is faithful and righteous to forgive us our sins and to cleanse us from all unrighteousness. If we say that we have not sinned, we make Him a liar and His word is not in us. 1 John 1:6-10 NASB

We start here because of the word faithful. We have stated that God is faithful. Without any question He is faithful and just to forgive our sins. The only question we need to now answer is why? Why is He faithful to us? The answer is in the above few verses of John 4:6-10.

It is important to know and remember that when the Scriptures were written they were letters, not divided into chapters and verses. With that in mind we must acknowledge that this passage is just shortly after our beginning point. Faithful and just to forgive us because God loves us. In verse ten God declares He sent His Son to be the propitiation for our sin. Webster defines propitiation in the second definition like this:

> To stand as an equivalent; to make reparation, amends or satisfaction for an offense or a crime, by which reconciliation is procured between the offended and offending parties.

Jesus is the one who sacrificed His Holy life for you and for me.

What is amazing here is that the love of God comes into play in His faithfulness. If you mess with me enough I stop being forgiving. Fool me once shame on you, fool me twice shame on me is the Americanized version of this activity. God, in His omniscient says I know when you are fooling, but I am still faithful and just to forgive. Because I love you, I sent My Son to die for your sins. God forgives and forgives and forgives. Faithful because He loves us and forgives our failings and sin.

I submit to you that you will not be faithful in your life commitments unless you truly love someone. I have been challenged by this problem many times in my life. Do I love my children enough to be faithful in my commitment to them? Or my wife? I had a scary experience years ago. I got on a plane owned and operated by a company that practices open seating. You sit where you can get a seat. It was a full flight and I was the last one on the plane. I had just had a very difficult time with the gate agent and one of the flight attendants. I had in my possession over $15,000.00 worth of electronic equipment. The equipment was packed in two cases for carry on. When I arrived at the door I was told one case had to go into the cargo hold of the plane. I was very upset. Such a bag would not be insured by the airline. As a result of being last, I had to sit next to a woman that became overly friendly. We talked a lot and had a nice visit, and when we parted at the baggage claim she gave me a hug and kiss. That had never happened to me before and that kiss seamed loaded with possibility. Now the question is do I react or do I keep my faithfulness intact with my wife?

While the text of 1 Corinthians 13 regarding loves does not come out and say in just so many words that love is faithful it is certainly implied in the context. Notice if you will in verses 4-8 what is said about love. Admittedly this is not everything in the text but it suffices for our needs:

Love:
    A. Suffers long.
    B. Does not parade itself.
    C. Does not seek its own.
    D. Does not rejoice in iniquity.
    E. Bears all things.
    F. Believes all things (in the one they love and trust).
    G. NEVER FAILS.

Love never fails the one who is loved. At that moment in that airport, I was faced with a huge choice. Pursue where whatever happened was going, or be faithful. It may be nothing was happening and it was satan working on me to get me to do something stupid, or it was satan working on two people to get them to do something stupid. I could have done something stupid or I could be faithful. I love my wife, so the decision was made long ago. I got out of there fast. I wish I could say that I always ran as fast from temptation as I did that day. In fact, I pray that I could run even faster. Love does not fail the one it loves. Love is faithful.

God, so loved the world, that he remains faithful to this day to forgive our sins. If we, as husbands, fathers, mothers, wives and children of God, love our spouses and family we remain faithful to them. Love does not fail.

You might say, "well, I know this person who claimed to be a Christian and they failed." Well, so do I; and it is often a very painful experience in the church world when these types of loses happen. I submit to you that they are the result of losing our first loves.

> 'But I have this against you, that you have left your first love. 'Therefore, remember from where you have fallen, and repent and do the deeds you did at first; or else I am coming to you and will remove your lampstand out of its place--unless you repent.
> Revelation 2:4-5 NASB

Here Jesus speaks to the church of Ephesus. He calls them to repentance because they have lost their first love and have sinned. Love forgives when failure happens, love restores, and love does not fail the fallen. Love is faithful to forgive, bear, endure and does not rejoice in iniquity. Love lets the errors be forgiven. Love is faithful to the standard of the cross; it is always faithful and just to forgive.

As we consider the world's reaction to failure we are puzzled at times. We see the guilty go free and the innocent found guilty in the court of public opinion. You never know which way the public's opinion will swing. And you find that even if people are truly repentant we don't forgive. We hold failure over their heads. We become unfaithful friends. We do not demonstrate faith in their repentance and we become unfaithful. We rationalize away our need to be faithful by simply stating that they will have to earn our trust. I am glad God doesn't treat me that way.

I will be the first to advocate that repentance must be genuine for me to be totally forgiving. And I will admit if I forgive you that I will watch your life to be certain I have not been duped. But, if I truly have love for you and want to be the faithful friend to you that I should be, or faithful spouse that I should be then I will communicate with you to be certain you are being supported as you grow out of your failure.

Rather than being faithful to forgive and help to grow or being faithful to our relationship with God and our spouse, satan would have us to be unfaithful; unfaithful to church, to family, then to our spouse, to our daily quiet time, and the list goes on and on. When we start becoming unfaithful in one area we grow increasingly weakened in the others. Without daily food I grow weak. Without spiritual food I grow weak. I once had a New Testament with a cute, "special imprint" cover on it in my office that said, "Food, if you don't eat food you become food." This is so true in the spiritual walk. If you want to be faithful, or develop any of these fruits you must eat deeply of God's Word, the Bible.

Faithfulness is perhaps the most important fruit as there are so many opportunities to be unfaithful to God that we must keep a strong relationship with God to remain faithful. To remain faithful to our spouse we must develop a strong relationship and nurture it as often and as much as possible.

SCRIPTURE ON FAITHFULNESS FOR REFLECTION

Deuteronomy 7:9

Psalms 31:23

Psalms 36:5

Psalms 40:10

Psalms 89

Psalms 92:2

Psalms119:90

Psalms 119:38

Proverbs 27:6

Isaiah 25:1

Isaiah 49:7

Lamentations 3:23

Matthew 25:21. 23

Luke 16:10

1 Corinthians 1:9

1 Corinthians 4:2

1 Corinthians 10:13

1 Thessalonians 5:24

2 Timothy 2:11

Titus 1:9

Hebrew 10:23

CHAPTER NINE

THE FRUIT OF MEEKNESS

"Come to Me, all who are weary and heavy-laden, and I will give you rest. 'Take My yoke upon you and learn from Me, for I am gentle and humble in heart, and YOU WILL FIND REST FOR YOUR SOULS. 'For My yoke is easy and My burden is light.'"

Matthew 11:28-30 NASB

Come unto me, all ye that labour and are heavy laden, and I will give you rest. Take my yoke upon you, and learn of me; for I am meek and lowly in heart: and ye shall find rest unto your souls. For my yoke is easy, and my burden is light.

Matthew 11:28-30 KJV

The subject of meekness is indeed one of the most difficult subjects of the Bible to discuss. Not that it should be, in fact, it should be one of the most discussed and readily accepted portions of the Christians life. However, in the current age of the church, meekness has taken it on the chin and is down for the count. Instead of meekness we hear about assertion, and building oneself up and of self-esteem. We hear much about the Christian as the powerful ones able to take on the world. We see Christians becoming socially active and taking on the courts, and we applaud their boldness. While some are genuine, others are self-seeking and looking only for the publicity, and attention that goes with being in the limelight. While we must realize that Christians need self-esteem, boldness, and that they need to be assertive in the proper situations, we must couple the teaching of these concepts with a solid introduction to meekness.

Meekness is more than just a word. When applied in its fullest measure it is the key to healthy self-esteem. Meekness is the attribute that will give the strength to be assertive in the proper situations, and will give the meek person the feeling of psychological well-being in spite of turmoil.

MEEKNESS AS AN ATTRIBUTE

The first thing we will notice when looking for Scriptural support for God as a God of meekness is that there are no Scriptures that deal with God directly. We do find two concerning Jesus that speak directly to meekness and we must recognize three things concerning Jesus and his relationship with God the Father. First, what Jesus saw the Father do, He did (John 5:19). Second, whoever saw Jesus has seen the Father (John 14:9). Thirdly, Jesus said "I and the Father are One" (John 10:30). We can then know that when we look at Christ we are seeing a true example of who God is, and His personality.

Let us then consider Matthew 11:28-30 from the introduction of this chapter. I have included both the NASB and the KJV translations of this passage. More and more modern translations use the word humble instead of meek when describing meekness. There is no problem with humility as a substitution for meekness. However, as we sideline the word meekness, I find meekness loses the power of the word when it is translated as humble.

Humility, in my mind, seems too often be retiring from conflict, meekness stands up to conflict in a gentle manner. We are taught to speak the truth in love

(Ephesians 4:15). In my understanding that is done in meekness and with authority.

Paul admonishes fathers not to provoke their children to anger. As parents we are not to be so harsh that we cause rebellion in our children. To accomplish this we need firm, meek discipline. Not harsh unreasonable discipline. Generally, the meek person will think before responding, will act rationally, and with compassion. Meekness should never be confused with weakness.

As we look to the great example, Jesus Christ, we see strength. He was not afraid of anything the enemy could do to Him. Yet in every situation, including cleansing the temple we see Him in total control of His emotions.

Webster's 1828 Dictionary puts it this way:
MEEK, a. [L. mucus; Eng. mucilage; Heb. to melt.]

1. Mild of temper; soft; gentle; not easily provoked or irritated; yielding; given to forbearance under injuries.

Now the man Moses was very meek, above all men. Numbers 12:3.

2. Appropriately, humble, in an evangelical sense; submissive to the divine will; not proud, self-sufficient or refractory; not peevish and apt to complain of divine dispensations. Christ says, "Learn of me, for I am meek and lowly in heart, and ye shall find rest to your souls." Matthew 11:29.

Blessed are the meek, for they shall inherit the earth.
Matthew 5:5.

The picture the world wants to paint of God is one of an ogre waiting for you and I to screw up so He can crush us. It is the picture that is portrayed to children when their parents allow ill-temper to control their actions instead of meekness.

Also let us consider Paul's writing to Corinth:

> *Now I, Paul, myself urge you by the meekness and gentleness of Christ--I who am meek when face to face with you, but bold toward you when absent!*
> *2 Corinthians 10:1 NASB*

I have shown here two verses of Scripture concerning the meekness of Christ; the first (at the beginning of this chapter) is an autobiographical statement from Christ; the second one (above) a testimonial from Paul. It is important to remember that Paul, even though he was not a close disciple of Christ, he was an observer of all that Christ did in his ministry. Paul, before conversion on the Damascus Road could have been among the crowds that watched Jesus perform miracles. I can almost see him at the temple office writing down the names of all who would transgress the Law of Moses by following this man, Jesus.

Paul knew all too well what he was up against in Jesus, he knew the man's character and his personality. So that after his conversion he could write about Christ as one who knew him intimately. He knew of the meekness of Christ. He knew that no matter what they did to ruffle his feathers, Jesus would answer them in a way that took the wind out of their sails and left them contemplating what was said. Paul knew His nature was gentle and meek.

We also have the autobiographical statement of Christ. We all can say things that are autobiographical, yet lack any support from our character. I can tell you that I am even tempered, but that would not be true all the time. I am just like you, stress me out and I get edgy and will lose patience. The difference between Jesus' statement and mine is that for Him it is true all the time for me it might be true today but tomorrow could change. Jesus is the same yesterday today and tomorrow (Hebrews 13:8). We must recognize that when Jesus Christ reveals Himself, He reveals God, for They are One.

For some it will be difficult to see God as meek. We want only to see Him as the judge of the wicked. We sometimes want to see Him as the all-powerful, ready to destroy, God. It is certain that to see God only as judgmental would play right into the hands of the enemy of our souls. If we only see and show God as the awesome, powerful, judgmental, vengeful God that some would see Him as, then we play right into the traps of the enemy to keep people from God. After all who in their right mind would want to hang around with a bully? That is the picture satan would paint for the world, God as a bully. But, God is not a bully; He is a just, loving, merciful, patient, God who is meek and lowly with his Son, Jesus Christ.

One of the great paradoxes of the Christian Faith is to see God both as awesome and just and all powerful, and then to see Him as meek, loving and merciful. Perhaps the only parallel we have that gives us an idea of God is the corporate executive. He wields awesome power over his employees, some of which the government and unions have whittled away at, but still a very powerful individual, yet as a person may be very gentle, kind, even meek. If he exhibits such characteristics, gentleness, kindness, etc., then he probably has very loyal employees.

If we can see God from this perspective we can also see Him as the loving Father of Romans 8:15 where we are able as Paul says to call Him, "Abba, Father." Then become aware of the reason individuals have been able to develop the intense loyalty that has given them the courage to even lay down their life for the cause of Christ. His meekness in dealing with our hearts deepens our resolve to serve and honor Him. Make no mistake, meekness is not weakness.

There is a quite strength in meekness. Meekness comes when you know that you have the power to destroy your enemy, whether with bombs or with words, but you would rather make a friend than to hurt them. That is how God has dealt with humanity for all time, and is how He deals with us now. He would rather have us as friends and adopted children than to destroy even one of us. Note what Peter writes about God's waiting:

> *The Lord is not slow about His promise, as some count slowness, but is patient toward you, not wishing for any to perish but for all to come to repentance.* 2 Peter 3:9 NASB

At any moment the end could come, yet God waits. Therefore, the final judgment waits, until He can wait no longer. This should be the message of the church when we talk of the end of the age. God is waiting to make your acquaintance, to love you and care for you. He does not desire to annihilate you.

We need to see God as the one who holds the power and chooses not to use it, but in gentleness comes to humanity and offers His love and a life everlasting with Him.

MEEKNESS AS AN EMOTIONAL RESPONSE

One of the most important areas of life that was quickly being overrun by the technology age we live in is the area of the individual self. People who worked for years on the same job for the same company were replaced by computer operated robots. More and more the automation and artificial intelligence of industry takes away from the sense of accomplishment. We no longer earn our living by the sweat of our brows, but by the cunningness of our minds. We pressure our children to learn in ways that we never experienced, and they are labeled learning disabled if they can't keep pace with the other children. We are expecting more and getting less. The high school graduate today has little hope of a profitable career unless they attend college. The college graduate needs a Master's Degree to get more than an entry level position in many fields. We put more pressure on students to learn, yet the raw score of the standardized tests continues to fall, and kids develop in one of two ways, a superiority complex, prideful, boastful, etc. or they feel inadequate. They lack self-worth.

How can meekness help? One, meekness can be the reassurance they need. Those who lack meekness often lack self-worth, so they proceed in socially unacceptable ways to tell you their value. It happens with teens, and children and adults. Our prisons are full of people that were trying to tell someone that they had value. They wanted to be recognized. The reason the cops can solve a case that left no leads is often the perpetrator of the crime can't keep their mouth shut about what they have done. They want someone to know about their accomplishment, and they are looking for acceptance; acceptance from anyone, even if it's another criminal.

Meekness, presented as an acceptable life style to a young child and demonstrated as a strong, careful, not haughty, determination to succeed no matter what the odds, type of characteristic, will give place for the formulation of the concept that it is more important to be seen as honorable than as obnoxious. Today we can see the result of a generation that has no concept of meekness as they howl and scream if they do get their own way.

Meekness is complimentary of the accomplishments of others. People are looking for acceptance. Meekness accepts them where they are because the meek person loves them as "they are" not foolishly with closed eyes but open eyes. They see things not as they are or they might be, but as they can be in Christ. One of the biggest mistakes we can make with our children is to fail to affirm their accomplishments. I know that some will disagree with me on the next illustration, but please read or listen to all that I am saying here. When my daughters came home with their grade cards I gave them money for each A or B that they had earned, more for A's than B's. Some would say that it is wrong to pay your children for getting grades, and that good grades are to be expected.

My argument is this; at the end of a week of work what do you expect from your employer? A pat on the back and congratulations for a job well done or a paycheck? The paycheck of course, and the pat on the back would be nice. We don't let children work to earn money; instead we send them to school. If someone in our society was paying the child to work the hours we send kids to school and make them do homework, we would take them to court for violating child labor laws. Instead we destroy their self-esteem and self-worth educating them and ignoring them.

In a defense mode they try to establish themselves in the adult world, they rebel and become proud and haughty and disruptive and we can't understand why. Meekness acknowledges the self-worth of the individual and provides for the development of their personal self-esteem.

Meekness is not weakness. It is instead the key to helping those around us develop into the full-bodied person that they can be. Meekness brings them into the body of Christ as they acknowledge through the meekness that is developed in them that they can be nothing without God. Parents that are always fighting and clawing at the system will have kids that are doing the same unless the child chooses to be different. Parents that have meekness and instill meekness in the child will succeed. There are those who confuse meekness with a crushed human spirit, but meekness is not, it is the human spirit in humbleness before God and loving and humble before humanity. The meek person knows that they can do all things through Christ who strengthens them. The crushed spirit does not know if they can go on. We tend not to differentiate between the two. We must teach and model meekness so that our children can become all that God intended us to be.

THE ANTITHESIS OF MEEKNESS

When pride comes, then comes dishonor, but with the humble is wisdom.   Proverbs 11:2 NASB

Pride goes before destruction, and a haughty spirit before stumbling. It is better to be humble in spirit with the lowly Than to divide the spoil with the proud.   Proverbs 16:18-19 NASB

An angry man stirs up strife, and a hot-tempered man abounds in transgression. A man's pride will bring him low, but a humble spirit will obtain honor.

Proverbs 29:22-23 NASB

As we look at the antithesis we will discover some things that can help foster self-esteem that will allow those around us to exhibit meekness.

Among the words that can be used as an antithesis for meekness are aggressive, assertive, and strong-willed. The definitions of these words use terms as forceful, outspoken, aggressive, forward, pushy, and belligerent. A common denominator of these terms is pride. Some might call it self-assured, but the self-assured do not have to present themselves in a negative way to be noticed. Each of these definers has negative overtones. They, in themselves, are not necessarily negative, but the common usage is recognized as negative. The common denominator is often pride used in inappropriate ways.

Self-esteem, the ability to feel good about yourself, is not pride. Self-esteem recognizes one's value and worth in relationship to their own shortfalls. It is possible to realize that you cannot be everything to everyone, and still have a good sense of who you are and what you can accomplish. Each one of us have specific abilities not shared by everyone else. I can do many things, but I cannot play the piano. My wife can play the piano, but she cannot change the brakes on a car. So, it is with many people around you and I, we can do things that others cannot. That fact does not give us license to behave in an unseemly manner. The antithesis of meekness says you are entitled. Meekness says it is not necessary to behave in spiteful ways.

The concern expressed here is about pride in its ugliest form. It is important to note that it is possible to be pleased with an accomplishment and to have good self-esteem. The person we are discussing here has low or non-existent self-esteem and has to compensate by the use of negative pride. It is important for the Christian to have a good sense of his value to God, and humanity. It is important for him to know that he has worth, and to accept that worth in the context of who God is within him. It is, however, unacceptable to be proud, haughty, boastful, and belligerent. It is also contrary to God's word.

MEEKNESS AND THE LOVE CONNECTION

Love is patient, love is kind and is not jealous; love does not brag and is not arrogant, does not act unbecomingly; it does not seek its own, is not provoked, does not take into account a wrong suffered, does not rejoice in unrighteousness, but rejoices with the truth; bears all things, believes all things, hopes all things, endures all things.
1 Corinthians 13:4-7 NASB

Let us turn our attention to Meekness and Love. I Corinthians 13:4 in the King James Version says, "Love vaunteth not itself, is not puffed up." Love is not prideful. Love does not go around telling you how great it is. For one thing we all know how great it is to be in love with someone else, or to be in love with God. You don't have to ask if a person is in love with someone else, it shows. It is really difficult to love or even be around someone who is "stuck on themselves."

There is a great chasm between the person who is self-assured and self-confident with meekness and the person who is just arrogantly and egotistically self-assured. The self-confident person who has meekness is not threatened by the success of others; in fact, they want you to succeed and are willing to share their knowledge with you so you might succeed. Then there is the self-confident person who is not interested in you, only your money, or in using you as a stepping stone to some greater personal gain. The problem with using people as stepping stones is when they have been crushed they don't hold up the weight as well as solid rocks do, and hence the walls start to crumble. People get tired of arrogance, and they move away from it, but people will support sincerity until the end.

In the realm of linking love and meekness no one does it better than Paul. As he writes to the church at Corinth, he chastises them concerning some error in the church. Then in chapter four of I Corinthians he tells them that he is coming for a visit when God will allow him. He states he will come either with the rod of correction or (I Corinthians 4:21) "...in love, and in the spirit of meekness?"

How do you wish to be dealt with? With love and meekness or with the rod of correction? My guess is meekness. We need to be sensitive to the pattern for correction that Paul uses in this portion of Scripture. Before he gets really punitive in his correction of them, he gives them the opportunity to choose for themselves how he will deal with them. There are occasions when parents need to move a little slower in the area of punishment and allow our older children the same option. This is not to say we should delay all punishments at all times, to do so would be to never punish. We must give opportunity for growth coupled with incentive.

Meekness is the quality that keeps us from seeking to destroy the things that we don't like, but are not necessarily contrary to God's Word. As my daughters grew up they were like every teenager, they got mad about things. Nothing really, just stuff that didn't go their way. I would quote Ephesians to them:

BE ANGRY, AND yet DO NOT SIN; do not let the sun go down on your anger. Ephesians 4:26 NASB

I would challenge them to decide if the thing that was causing the anger was going to have an effect on eternity. Was it worth the energy they were spending? I would usually get an answer of "no it wasn't." I would suggest that we could change the situation faster with understanding and thoughtfulness rather than anger. I simply employed the basic you can catch more flies with honey than vinegar approach.

People that have learned to love with the agape love of Christ know that in meekness there is a power to change the opinions of people, even in the most challenging situations. When you or I try to take things by force we will always meet resistance. When we have rational calm discussions, we are able to work out solutions. Meekness, that comes from a base of love for individuals, will find the place for such discussions.

Sometimes meekness looks weak. It cannot be helped, but a quiet resolve founded in meekness will never be over run and destroyed. There has since the time of Christ been countless martyrs for the cause of Christ. The act of not submitting to the demand of renouncing their faith, but in meekness standing firm in their faith has led to revivals time and time again among the people who chose martyrdom over life.

We are living in a time when Christians and Christian values are under attack from the media, the courts in some cases, certainly at the state, federal and local government levels in many states. How Christians react and act in light of the attacks will be recorded for the world to review, and see if we exhibited the fruit of the Spirit, to determine if we are Christians of the Word.

How will your story be written? Will it be said you were meek and loving or something else?

SCRIPTURE ON MEEKNESS/GENTLENESS FOR REFLECTION

Numbers 12:3	*Zephaniah 2:3*
2 Samuel 22:36	*Matthew 5:5*
Psalms 22:26	*Matthew 11:29*
Psalms 25:9	*I Corinthians 4:21*
Psalms 37:11	*Colossians 3:12*
Psalms 76:9	*Titus 3:2*
Psalms 147:6	*James 1:21*
Psalms 149:4	*James 3:13*
Isaiah 29:19	*1 Peter 3:4, 15*
Isaiah 61:1	

CHAPTER TEN

THE FRUIT OF TEMPERANCE

Now the deeds of the flesh are evident, which are: immorality, impurity, sensuality, idolatry, sorcery, enmities, strife, jealousy, outbursts of anger, disputes, dissensions, factions, envying, drunkenness, carousing, and things like these, of which I forewarn you, just as I have forewarned you, that those who practice such things will not inherit the kingdom of God.   Galatians 5:19-21 NASB

At the first mention of the word temperance, almost without exception those that are old enough, will remember the Women's Christian Temperance Union[1] (WCTU or WWTU) will think in terms of stopping people from drinking alcoholic beverages. Others will think in terms of prohibiting from alcohol. The major drawback of having associated temperance with alcoholic beverages is that it constrains the concept of temperance, and makes it of almost no effect among Conservative Evangelicals. We who make up this group of Christians, especially among the Pentecostals, and in some cases the Charismatic's are perfectly willing to allow temperance to mean "abstinence from alcohol."

Abuses include things like our caloric intake, (excessive weight issues), bulimia/anorexia, hoarding, compulsive buying, compulsive giving, never being able to say no, etc. The list is long.

The problem that this has created is that we often see members of the body of Christ who look like anything but well-tuned soldiers fit for battle. Instead they are less than battle ready. They are unprepared in every sense of the word. But lest you think I am talking about just weight think again because to go into battle takes mental preparedness as well as physical preparedness. We must accept the fact that temperance is more than not drinking alcohol. It is self-discipline, self-control, and moderation in all things, showing evidence of self-denial, self-restraint, and cautious Christian behavior. It is overcoming temptation.

No temptation has overtaken you but such as is common to man; and God is faithful, who will not allow you to be tempted beyond what you are able, but with the temptation will provide the way of escape also, so that you will be able to endure it.
1 Corinthians 10:13 NASB

It has taken me a long time to recognize this truth. Self-control, or temperance is about overcoming temptation. When food is calling my name, I am tempted to over eat. When I want to lash out at someone in uncontrolled anger, temptation is calling my name. If it is of a sexual nature that is not within the confines of marriage, temptation is calling. If it is to shove the gas pedal all the way to the floor and see what that car will really do, temptation is calling my name. Temptation calls to each one of us in the weakest area of our lives.

An evangelist friend once told me that more than 80% of the pastors he ministered with in over 40 years of ministry had confessed to him they struggled regularly with sexual temptation. That is not to say they gave place to the temptation it is only to acknowledge they are subject to the attack of the enemy like everyone else.

We can no longer afford to look through rose colored glasses; we must look at this body of Christ and realize too often we are out of shape soldiers, we are not ready for battle. Allow me to use a metaphor of a sleeping giant to describe the church today and the battle for the church's survival in 21st century America.

It would seem that there are two ways to fight a war, one is with words and subtle deeds, and the other is a forceful attack. Using the first requires subtlety; never enough activity to arouse the sleeping giant. Never enough to get people stirred up. Aggravated, yes, but not angry; never stirred into action, just occasionally miffed. And when you find one making too many waves, you silence them any way you can, but best of all by disgracing them in front of their peers and followers. This then allows the sleeping giant to turn over and go back to sleep. This tactic is used over and over by the media and some politicians today.

The other, the forceful and direct way to fight is the all-out frontal attack. Not always a popular way to fight and often a very poor choice in winning. It angers the opponent and sets off a series of counter attacks measured to reject the frontal attack. If the giant is too far out of shape the war is soon over, but if there is still some signs of preparedness and stability then time will bring the giant into the fighting shape ready to win the battle.

The bride of Christ is a sleeping giant, and she lacks temperance as she indulges in those things which keep her unprepared for battle, and she ignores the little skirmishes around her, allowing the battles to be lost. The fruit of self-control or temperance, is nearly lost on the church today. We spend too much time with our cell phones, too much time on our computers surfing the internet, too much time playing video/computer games, too much time watching TV, and too much time eating to excess.

Years ago, I belonged to a Toastmasters Club[2] in Kansas City. Toastmasters is about enhancing your public speaking skills and I still belong to a club today. I enjoy the challenge and the benefits of the club. I mention this because one of the best speeches I ever heard was at a Kansas City Toastmasters Meeting entitled "Enough, but not too much." The theme of the speech was that we need to enjoy life, but overdoing anything was counterproductive. Too much food results in damage to your health. Too much alcohol, damage to your liver, health and potentially life around you and your relationships. Too much religion was mentioned, with the caveat never too much relationship with God and the Son, but too much church to the neglect of family responsibilities was detrimental. "Enough, but not too much." Pretty well said in my opinion, and that is the message of temperance.

Before I go on with this section I need to confess this is the one area of my life I struggle with. I am a closet over eater. I have almost no self-control when it comes to food. As a result of writing this chapter and having to come face to face with my own issue, I have enlisted a friend to be my conscious. We both need to lose weight and are compulsive eaters, we are checking on each other to help us stand tall in the light of our weakness.

We can be strong in so many areas, but then we find that we have struggles in one area. It is not my intention that any part of this book would condemn, but instead bring hope that we can overcome, and we will overcome by the blood of the lamb and the word of our testimony. (Revelation 12:11). It has taken me almost two months to get to this chapter because of the struggle I am engaged in regarding my eating habits. I have promised myself that I will do better so many times that it is a hollow promise, so today I decided to do better and it is with God's help that I will. I want to be a fully formed fruit bearing person.

Having said this let us look at temperance as an attribute.

TEMPERANCE AS AN ATTRIBUTE

"For I, the LORD, do not change; therefore you, O sons of Jacob, are not consumed.
Malachi 3:6 NASB

Every good thing given and every perfect gift is from above, coming down from the Father of lights, with whom there is no variation or shifting shadow.
James 1:17 NASB

In this section we will look at the unchanging God we serve and His instructions to us about self-discipline.

It is important to note that there is no Scripture that says God is self-controlled, but there are several that give us insight to the God that never changes.

One of the notable things about self-controlled people is that for them self-control/self-discipline always does things a certain way. They always get up in the morning to walk three miles. They always get to the gym to work out. They always wear the same size, and weigh about the same amount. They are always at the top of the class, and on and on and on. The self-disciplined person is always just about the same in everything and every way, day in and day out, year after year. We have all known a few people like that. You can count on them and count on their reaction to any given stimuli.

God is like that; He is the Lord, and He does not change, in Him there is no variation. The two verses I began this section with are two favorites from Scripture. They state that God, never changes and His ways are not varied but constantly the same.

The correct theological term for this unchanging God is immutability. God is immutable; absolutely unchangeable. A lot of things undergo mutation, but God is immutable. He does not change. He exhibits the ultimate in self-disciple; the ultimate in self-control. If He didn't our universe would have spun out of control long ago and you might not have been born. It would have destroyed our ancestors hundreds of years ago.

We all have areas we are fighting to gain control of in our lives, whether it is food, drugs, TV, cigarettes, booze, pornography, driving on the edge, clothes buying, frivolous spending, or just fill in the blank. We all have an area of our lives we wish we had more control of, but God is always in control. He is never intemperate. He always is and remains the same. Jesus shares this quality with the Father, Hebrews 13:8 reminds us that "Jesus Christ is the same, yesterday, today and forever."

TEMPERANCE AS AN EMOTION

I have thought long and hard about self-control as an emotion. When we lose control, we get emotional in one of two ways, either anger or guilt. Sometimes the anger is first, followed by the guilt.

When we lose control lots of emotions appear, and not just in us. We anger others, we cause them to fear for their safety. We can destroy love and turn it into hate or apathy. So much happens emotionally at the loss of self-control that lives are impacted whether we wanted them to be or not.

As to whether this is an emotion or emotional response the loss of self-control can definitely result in emotion. We get overwhelmed with a situation and then we react. The question is do we react in a Christ like manner or not? When we act in ways not consistent with Scripture we are out of line and not showing the Fruit of the Spirit to the world.

Please look at the reading list for this chapter, it is near the end. I attempted to gather together some of the Scriptural characteristics we should exhibit in times of difficulty. When temptation comes to really lose it, I hope you will take time to check out what the Bible says and then take some time to reflect and think about the Word. A wonderful word that is Biblical but has been hijacked by so many false religions is meditate. David said in Psalm 1 to meditate on God's Word. May I suggest that is what we need to do when we face the challenges of self-control.

THE ANTITHESIS OF TEMPERANCE

Quite honestly the long and the short of the antithesis is this, out of control. It may manifest as irrational anger, drunkenness, overweight, (and not all overweight people are lacking in self-control for some it is medical condition), overindulgent, slovenly. That is just the tip of a huge ice berg, but why are these the opposite of self-control. There is but one thing to describe it "giving into temptation."

We say, "well, I really shouldn't, but..." I've only had one, two, three... or I can afford to cheat I was good earlier today; I will skip...later, I will go to the gym this week, and we rationalize our intemperate behavior with clichés we have used and heard a thousand times over.

What we really are doing is failing to respond to the temptations that violate our Christian walk. Food is the most offensive of all the things we can talk about when it comes to self-control because we all have to eat. We can justify our actions when it comes to eating, but it is not so easy with drugs and alcohol, and other areas of intemperance.

The enemy of your soul uses anything he can to get you to feel bad about yourself. When I look in a mirror and see the extra weight I carry I get down, when I get down I don't function as well as I should, and I eat. The problem begets the problem and there is only one way to break the cycle. It is found in resisting temptation.

TEMPERANCE AND THE LOVE CONNECTION

Love...Doth not behave itself unseemly, seeketh not her own, is not easily provoked, thinketh no evil;
1 Corinthians 13:5 KJV

Love does not behave itself unseemly ... (I Cor. 13:5) other translations render this unbecomingly, ill-mannered, disgracefully, indecently or rude. One says conceited. Allow us, if you will, to think in terms of this: "love does not act in any way that is contrary to the word of God, whether on the personal level or interpersonal level." The person without self-control is going to say things he/she should not, and they will be injurious to another. They are going to do things he/she should not, and it will be insulting to others. In general, the person who does not bring the body into the subjection of God and His love will do just about anything that he/she wishes no matter who it hurts, no matter how rude or arrogant it might be.

Love does not behave itself in such a way. Love is considerate, allowing others to go first. Romans 12:10 states; "Be kindly affectionate one to another with brotherly love, in honor giving preference to one another." In other words, love others, be in self-control and let other Christians be first. With love, don't think only of yourself, but of others. Don't let intemperance, the greed and lusts of the flesh, so rule your life that you forget about other people.

> *For you are all sons of light and sons of day. We are not of night nor of darkness; so then let us not sleep as others do, but let us be alert and sober. For those who sleep do their sleeping at night, and those who get drunk get drunk at night. But since we are of the day, let us be sober, having put on the breastplate of faith and love, and as a helmet, the hope of salvation.*
>
> I Thessalonians 5:5-8NASB

The NIV uses the word self-controlled in this passage, but let us realize that to be sober minded is not to be un-drunk but to act with clarity of mind. Alcohol clouds the thinking and impairs the judgment and to be sober minded is to be thinking without the impairment of anything clouding the mind. We often say things like "what was I thinking of" when we discover we have made a silly or stupid mistake. We didn't have to be drunk to make such a mistake only not thinking clearly.

Be of sober spirit, be on the alert. Your adversary, the devil, prowls around like a roaring lion, seeking someone to devour. 1 Peter 5:8 NASB

Paul also writes to us in Corinthians:

Do you not know that those who run in a race all run, but only one receives the prize? Run in such a way that you may win. Everyone who competes in the games exercises self-control in all things. They then do it to receive a perishable wreath, but we an imperishable. Therefore, I run in such a way, as not without aim; I box in such a way, as not beating the air; but I discipline my body and make it my slave, so that, after I have preached to others, I myself will not be disqualified.
1 Corinthians 9:24-27 NASB

Paul's writing to the Galatians admonishes:

Now those who belong to Christ Jesus have crucified the flesh with its passions and desires. If we live by the Spirit, let us also walk by the Spirit. Let us not become boastful, challenging one another, envying one another. Galatians 5:24-26 NASB

Our humanity can get in between us and our Savior so easily that we often fail to recognize the symptoms. It is difficult to be temperate at a feast. One of the major holidays of our county, and one that was begun to honor God have turned into a feast rivaled only by a Roman orgy. We lose all bearings of temperance at Thanksgiving in respect to food. A month later we celebrate the birth of our Lord, Jesus Christ and we again lose all sense of temperance and we indulge in spending that sets new records almost yearly, and sets new debt levels for millions of Americans. But we justify it by saying we are giving gifts; when in fact we are often teaching our children intemperance concerning finances. A truly sad part of this is we get the list from the kids that we do our shopping from, and we reinforce the idea of intemperance.

As we look at the down side of temperance we realize that it involves every area of the flesh. Paul gives us a very clear picture in Galatians of the complex nature of the problem.

> *Now the deeds of the flesh are evident, which are: immorality, impurity, sensuality, idolatry, sorcery, enmities, strife, jealousy, outbursts of anger, disputes, dissensions, factions, envying, drunkenness, carousing, and things like these, of which I forewarn you, just as I have forewarned you, that those who practice such things will not inherit the kingdom of God.* Galatians 5:19-21 NASB

Paul also gives us a second excellent passage of Scripture in answer to these problems:

> *Therefore, consider the members of your earthly body as dead to immorality, impurity, passion, evil desire, and greed, which amounts to idolatry. For it is because of these things that the wrath of God will come upon the sons of disobedience, and in them you also once walked, when you were living in them. But now you also, put them all aside: anger, wrath, malice, slander, and abusive speech from your mouth. Do not lie to one another, since you laid*

aside the old self with its evil practices, and have put on the new self who is being renewed to a true knowledge according to the image of the One who created him-- a renewal in which there is no distinction between Greek and Jew, circumcised and uncircumcised, barbarian, Scythian, slave and freeman, but Christ is all, and in all. So, as those who have been chosen of God, holy and beloved, put on a heart of compassion, kindness, humility, gentleness and patience; bearing with one another, and forgiving each other, whoever has a complaint against anyone; just as the Lord forgave you, so also should you. Beyond all these things put on love, which is the perfect bond of unity.

Colossians 3:5-14 NASB

And Titus

Older men are to be temperate, dignified, sensible, sound in faith, in love, in perseverance.

Titus 2:2 NASB

Perhaps the best final thought on this fruit is found in Romans:

So then, brethren, we are under obligation, not to the flesh, to live according to the flesh-- for if you are living according to the flesh, you must die; but if by the Spirit you are putting to death the deeds of the body, you will live. For all who are being led by the Spirit of God, these are sons of God.

Romans 8:12-14 NASB

SCRIPTURE ON TEMPERANCE/SELF-CONTROL FOR REFLECTION

Exodus 34:6

Nehemiah 9:17

Psalm 103:8

Psalm 145:8

Proverbs 14:29

Proverbs 15:18

Proverbs 16:32

Joel 2:13

Jonah 4:2

Nahum 1:3

1 Corinthians 7:5

1 Corinthians 9:25

2 Peter 1:6.

James 1:1

CHAPTER ELEVEN

TOOLS FOR SHARING THE CHRISTIAN LIFE

What Tools are in Your Tool Box?

*For through the grace given to me I say to everyone
among you not to think more highly of himself than
he ought to think; but to think so as to have sound
judgment, as God has allotted to each a measure of
faith. For just as we have many members in one
body and all the members do not have the same
function, so we, who are many, are one body in
Christ, and individually members one of another.
Since we have gifts that differ according to the grace
given to us, each of us is to exercise them
accordingly: if prophecy, according to the proportion
of his faith; if service, in his serving; or he who
teaches, in his teaching; or he who exhorts, in his
exhortation; he who gives, with liberality; he who
leads, with diligence; he who shows mercy, with
cheerfulness.*

Romans 12:3-8 NASB

In this chapter I want to address the need to share your
new found, or perhaps your long ago found faith in Jesus
as Lord and Savior. No doubt someone encouraged you to
share your faith as a way to keep it strong when you first
accepted Christ. If they did not, let me encourage you to
do just that. We are overcomers when we share the word
of our testimony according to Revelation 12:11

Sometimes it is difficult to know what to share in terms
of our faith in Jesus. I want to ask you to consider what it
was that drew you to Christ? In the next few pages I am

going to list several items I call "Tools for sharing the Christian Life."

I use the metaphor of tools as I am a "jack of all trades, master of none" sort of person. I fix things, I wear a t-shirt that says Papa Can Fix-all proudly. There is a reason my kids call me when they have a problem. I either have the correct tool or know how to fix whatever the problem is with the tools I have. In my garage is a large assortment of tool boxes. More than 25 tool boxes; not to mention I have three rolling tool boxes.

Often when we talk about Spiritual tools in the church world it focuses on the weapons of our warfare. You need to quickly become familiar with the big three tools:

1. The Bible
2. Prayer as Spiritual Warfare
3. The Gifts of the Spirit

These are the "BIG THREE" and I don't want you to forget that. I have thought about the big three tools that I own; my hammer, my vise grips, and a multi-head screw driver. But there are a lot of tools I use regularly as well. Sockets, box-end and open-end wrenches, impact tools, it is a long list. Some tools are general use tools, some are specialty tools. The list found here includes both. The lower the number the more general the tool.

Here are the tools I see in the Christians tool box. They are in reverse order. I start with the least and move to the ones I feel are most important. My reason is simple. I want to leave the last three ringing in your heart as you finish this book.

13. Prophecy

This is the only gifting that Paul repeats in 1 Corinthians 12. A Pastor friend, John Elliot gave an indication that Claudia (his wife) might have this gift when she spoke to the kids. In a recent Sunday message, he shared that she was not interested in what had happened, but she was going to tell the children what was going to happen. Mr. Hanke, my eighth grade English teacher thought he was prophetic when he announced to the class one day that if you would "stick with Mixer, (me) and one day you too could wear a ball and chain."

There is much to be said about prophecy, but it is a discussion best had as it relates to the Gifts or Manifestations of the Spirit. I encourage you to read Martin Perryman's book *The Helper*[1] for a complete discussion on the subject.

The prophetic or spoken word can help a person see the error of the path they are on, or encourage them to seek a renewed or new relationship with Christ. Mr. Hanke did that for me, it changed my life's trajectory.

12. Service

Now as they were traveling along, He entered a village; and a woman named Martha welcomed Him into her home. She had a sister called Mary, who was seated at the Lord's feet, listening to His word. But Martha was distracted with all her preparations; and she came up to Him and said, "Lord, do You not care that my sister has left me to do all the serving alone? Then tell her to help me." But the Lord answered and said to her, "Martha, Martha, you are worried and bothered about so many things; but only one thing is necessary, for

Mary has chosen the good part, which shall not be taken away from her. "
Luke 10:38-42 NASB

The church world tends to pick on the Biblical Martha because she was off in the kitchen preparing to serve the Lord with physical ministrations. Today in the church there are few who want to be Martha's, but I submit to you that serving is an important tool in the tool box of the Christian.

There have been times in my life when I could not do for myself. After my last back surgery, I was in a body cast. I could not take it off or put it on by myself. I could not care for myself in the bathroom. I was in that cast for the better part of four months. There were people I had to depend upon, and I thanked God for their service to me. There are people all around you today who could use a few minutes of your time in service to them and the Lord. Doing it without asking speaks volumes about the Love of Christ within you and is a witness and testimony of your faith and relationship to God through Christ Jesus.

There are opportunities at nursing homes, elementary schools, middle schools, high schools, soup kitchens, rescue ministries, prisons, and you can add to that list just from your own life. It might be a neighbor that needs a helping hand and by doing so you show the love of Jesus Christ. The phrase "Random Acts of Kindness" needs to be a theme of our Christian tool box. Even a glass of water given in Jesus Name, an act of kindness and service can lead to a salvation.

"For whoever gives you a cup of water to drink because of your name as followers of Christ, truly I say to you, he will not lose his reward.
Mark 9:41 NASB

11. Hospitality

> Let love be without hypocrisy. Abhor what is evil; cling to what is good. Be devoted to one another in brotherly love; give preference to one another in honor; not lagging behind in diligence, fervent in spirit, serving the Lord; rejoicing in hope, persevering in tribulation, devoted to prayer, contributing to the needs of the saints, practicing hospitality.   Romans 12:9-21 NASB

A friend of mine and I were talking between services one Sunday about our home state of Minnesota. In MN you might get asked over for a "little lunch" following a church service. A little lunch in MN is like a seven-course meal. Goodbyes take a half hour or longer and you always leave with a few snacks for the ride home.

Maybe you're not the type to invite people to your home, but you like to go out on Sunday after church. Why not invite someone to join you? Or make plans to have dinner out during the week or weekend. There are so many ways to practice hospitality. Perhaps you have friends visiting the area, have them stay with you. Eat lots of pizza and Chinese takeout if you don't like to cook. A holiday season is always coming up, have a favorite food you make? Make an extra and share it with a neighbor.

Along with sharing the time in hospitality is the opportunity to share Jesus. You will never lead anyone to Christ unless you talk to non-Christians. Hospitality is one of the best ways to get to talk to the unsaved.

10. Leadership

Not everyone is a recognized "leader," but everyone should lead someone. If you have children you will lead their development, or they will be uncontrollable. If you work with people, you can be a leader just by doing the best job possible. Lead your department in sales, contacts, phone calls. Something, anything. Then use that position of leadership to share Jesus. I get excited when I hear an award winner on television say, "I want to thank my Lord and Savior Jesus Christ for this award\win\accolade.

They are not necessarily a great leader, but when the opportunity arises they lead. You can too. It is a tool in your tool box. Lead your grandchildren in prayer, even when and if their parents are not serving the Lord. My oldest grandson used to question me when I would pray for the day as we left for school. For a time, he would get mad at me for praying. I never stopped. Recently he was the one leading his little brother in prayer for dinner. Lead. Don't be afraid.

> *"If it is disagreeable in your sight to serve the LORD, choose for yourselves today whom you will serve: whether the gods which your fathers served which were beyond the River, or the gods of the Amorites in whose land you are living; but as for me and my house, we will serve the LORD."* Joshua 24:15 NASB

A friend of mine preached a sermon based on Joshua 1. Here are the verses:

> *"Be strong and courageous, for you shall give this people possession of the land which I swore to their fathers to give them. "Only be strong and very courageous; be careful to do according to all the law*

which Moses My servant commanded you; do not turn from it to the right or to the left, so that you may have success wherever you go." Joshua 1:6-7 NASB

He narrowed it down to two words. He heard them in a commercial years ago. "Do It." Be a leader in some way or about something and use the opportunity to glorify God and share your faith. *Just Do It.*

9. Teaching:

I have heard the following many times when asking people to be a part of the Sunday School program in the churches I have served. "I am not a teacher."

While it is true you may not be gifted to stand in front of adults to teach, if you are a Christian and you have a voice, you can teach. It is one of the greatest tools you can have in your tool box. Want to help a child read, get a Bible Story Book and teach them to read. Want to help a young person, find out their interests, if you have interests that are similar, share them, and find ways to interweave the Bible in your common experience. Use photography...the beauty of creation and a creative God. Use a computer and explain they work from logic and order, like the logic and order of the universe. Are automobiles and mechanics your thing? Talk about the oil of the Holy Spirit. Is cooking your passion, share the story of the woman and the small portion of flour, or the ravens feeding Elijah. Football, the game of your life? Talk about the "Game of Life." Does music drive who you are? Speak of David and the Psalms, learn a Psalm or ten that have been set to music, talk about the church's influence in classical hymns, Christian Songs, Contemporary artists.

Be careful what you teach. Examine the lyrics first. The beautiful song "Hallelujah, by Leonard Cohen contains this line "But all I've ever learned from love was how to shoot somebody who outdrew you[2]."

That may not be the legacy you want from your teaching.

8. Exhortation:

From Webster's Dictionary
EXHORTA'TION, n. The act or practice of exhorting; the act of inciting to laudable deeds; incitement to that which is good or commendable.
1. The form of words intended to incite and encourage.
2. Advice; counsel.

We seem to think of an exhorter as someone standing on a street corner telling people what they are doing is wrong. We don't think in terms of praise for the individual as an exhortation. Do you think your Pastor did a great job with their sermon last Sunday? Did you tell them so? The exhorter said more than just "Good Message, or Great Job." The exhorter got specific, I really enjoyed...I really understood that passage for the first time...I was convicted when you talked about. That is exhortation. It is positive and specific.

To exhort is to be specific. I paint a car and you say to me, nice paint, shiny, or such, I know that. Tell me you looked it over and there is no orange peel, the color is unique, ask how I got that shading, then I know you paid attention and I feel lifted by your praise. Nice job is nice, but say what you like about the job and you move to exhortation. You can exhort non-Christians too. In fact, telling someone what you liked, and why, can open a door for conversation that may lead to a friendship that will give you opportunity to share Christ.

If you have the opportunity to share a wisdom, to provide counsel, do it with a prayer for success in the endeavor. It opens the door to witness and allows for growth in Christ. We have so many nay-sayers in this world and in life we need Christian exhorters to rise up and encourage people, to appreciate their endeavors, to support them in their good works.

One of my favorite verses in the Bible is in Hebrews:

> *Let us hold fast the confession of our hope without wavering, for He who promised is faithful; and let us consider how to stimulate (the King James here says PROVOKE) one another to love and good deeds, not forsaking our own assembling together, as is the habit of some, but encouraging one another; and all the more as you see the day drawing near.*
>
> Hebrews 10:23-25 NASB

7. Importunity

> *Then He said to them, "Suppose one of you has a friend, and goes to him at midnight and says to him, 'Friend, lend me three loaves; for a friend of mine has come to me from a journey, and I have nothing to set before him'; and from inside he answers and says, 'Do not bother me; the door has already been shut and my children and I are in bed; I cannot get up and give you anything.' "I tell you, even though he will not get up and give him anything because he is his friend, yet because of his persistence {King James uses the word importunity here} he will get up and give him as much as he*

needs. *"So, I say to you, ask, and it will be given to you; seek, and you will find; knock, and it will be opened to you. "For everyone who asks, receives; and he who seeks, finds; and to him who knocks, it will be opened.*

Luke 11:5-10 NASB

I like the word importunity. I know it means persistent, but persistent reminds me of a little kid asking, "Why?" After a while you just want to put some duct tape over their tiny little mouths. Importunity is the grown-up version of "Why?" or Please. Thomas Edison was asked why he kept trying all the different substances to make the light bulb, he answered something like this, "I have not failed. I've just found 10,000 ways that won't work." Because of importunity we have electric light in its many forms today,

Importunity sees wrong and works to right it until it is righted. Importunity sees a soul worth saving and prays and reaches out until the soul is touched for the cause of Christ. Importunity says never give up, never surrender. Importunity says I didn't get healed today but there is tonight and tomorrow. Importunity says "though He slays me yet will I trust Him" (Job 13:15). Importunity says the gates of hell will not prevail against me I'll fight on the Lord's side. (Matthew 16:18)

There are several examples in the Bible of the importune. Abraham and Sarah. Yes, they got side tracked and tried to help God out, but in the end, they believed until Isaac was born. In Luke 2.25 we see Simeon. He hung in there until Jesus showed up. Anna did the same. Hannah, the mother of Samuel is another.

There is a little old widow woman in New Prague, MN by the name of Myra Goble. Myra told me on several occasions that the Lord promised her that she would be alive to see His return. She has been telling people that very same thing for probably 50 years or more. She does not give up in the telling. Here is the thing, she is in her 90's. If she is right the time is short, if she is wrong she will go to her grave believing in the imminent return of Christ. She is importune.

Put importunity in your Spiritual tool box. Teach it to new Christians, teach it to Children, and teach it to old Christians again and again. Paul likens the Christian walk to a race. He forgot to say a marathon race.

6. Mercy   5. Humility   4. Justice

These last three are basic Christian, Godliness requirements. These are not optional tools in your tool box. These you must have if you wish to be a witness of what Christ has done for you. Here are the Scripture verses related to the last three:

> *He has told you, O man, what is good; And what does the Lord require of you but to do justice, to love kindness (mercy KJV), And to walk humbly with your God?*
>
> Micah 6:8 NASB

For some reason I don't remember ever hearing a sermon on these three as a child or young person. My suspicion is that as a Pentecostal church we relegated these three to the mainstream churches. Much to my chagrin I did not speak on these in the early years of my ministry. We were taught to preach the New Testament as we were "New Testament" churches. That changed for me when as a youth pastor my young people were learning Romans for quizzing. We had pretty good quiz teams in those days and I was able to learn a lot with the kids, even as a graduate of a Bible College. The verse that got me was in Romans:

Do we then nullify the Law through faith? May it never be! On the contrary, we establish the Law.

Romans 3:31 NASB

6. Mercy

"The quality of mercy is not strained.
It droppeth as the gentle rain from heaven
Upon the place beneath. It is twice blessed:
It blesseth him that gives and him that takes.
'Tis mightiest in the mightiest. It becomes
The throned monarch better than his crown.
His scepter shows the force of temporal power,
The attribute to awe and majesty
Wherein doth sit the dread and fear of kings,
But mercy is above this sceptered sway.
It is enthroned in the hearts of kings.
It is an attribute to God himself.
And earthly power doth then show likest God's
When mercy seasons justice.
Therefore, Jew, though justice be thy plea, consider this,
That in the course of justice none of us
Should see salvation. We do pray for mercy,
And that same prayer doth teach us all to render
The deeds of mercy. I have spoken thus much
To mitigate the justice of thy plea,
Which if thou follow, this strict court of Venice
Must needs give sentence against the merchant there."
— William Shakespeare, The Merchant of Venice[3]

The gift of mercy is not overused is Shakespeare's point. It is not strained, it needs to be used. We are sometimes too quick to judge negatively. React with vengeance towards those who anger us.

I have a real problem with drivers that do dumb things. I don't have a lot of tolerance or patience. I also struggle with people who think they should be first no matter the needs of other people. I get frustrated with people who attempt to rip me off. Put both together in a matter of minutes and I am not going to show the greatest amount of mercy and grace. You would be hard pressed to find any anywhere within this person. I always have to repent later because even though I seldom unleash on people I fail as a Christian when I do. So do you!

Here is the point, instead of using a delicate tool like mercy, I grab the hammer of judgement. A hammer is a fine tool, for its intended purpose, but using a hammer to remove a bolt just doesn't work, and you end up frustrated. I have had to learn to use tools properly for them to be of value. It is the same with our Spiritual Tools. Mercy is one of the most important tools we have as Christians.

Webster gives us this in the 1828 edition. It is rather lengthy but speaks to the heart of mercy.

MER'CY, n. [L. misericordia.]
1. That benevolence, mildness or tenderness of heart which disposes a person to overlook injuries, or to treat an offender better than he deserves; the disposition that tempers justice, and induces an injured person to forgive trespasses and injuries, and to forbear punishment, or inflict less than law or justice will warrant. In this sense, there is perhaps no word in our language precisely

synonymous with mercy. That which comes nearest to it is grace. It implies benevolence, tenderness, mildness, pity or compassion, and clemency, but exercised only towards offenders. Mercy is a distinguishing attribute of the Supreme Being.

2. An act or exercise of mercy or favor. It is a mercy that they escaped.

3. Pity; compassion manifested towards a person in distress.

4. Clemency and bounty.

5. Charity, or the duties of charity and benevolence.

6. Grace; favor.

7. Eternal life, the fruit of mercy.

8. Pardon.

9. The act of sparing, or the forbearance of a violent act expected. The prisoner cried for mercy.

To be or to lie at the mercy of, to have no means of self-defense, but to be dependent for safety on the mercy or compassion of another, or in the power of that which is irresistible; as, to be at the mercy of a foe, or of the waves.

Webster's cites several Scripture verses in the definition. Here is the list:

The LORD is longsuffering, and of great mercy, forgiving iniquity and transgression...
Numbers 14:18 KJV

I am not worthy of the least of all the mercies, and of all the truth, which thou hast shewed unto thy servant; for with my staff I passed over this Jordan; and now I am become two bands. Genesis 32:10 KJV

And he said, He that shewed mercy on him. Then said Jesus unto him, Go, and do thou likewise.
Luke 10:37 KJV

Mercy and truth preserve the king: and his throne is upheld by mercy. Proverbs 20:28 KJV.

He that follows after righteousness and mercy finds life, righteousness, and honor. Proverbs 21:21 KJV

But go ye and learn what that means, I will have mercy, and not sacrifice: for I am not come to call the righteous, but sinners to repentance.
Matthew 9:13 KJV

5. Humility

"Whoever exalts himself shall be humbled; and whoever humbles himself shall be exalted.
Matthew 23:12 NASB

But He gives a greater grace. Therefore, it says, "GOD IS OPPOSED TO THE PROUD, BUT GIVES GRACE TO THE HUMBLE."
James 4:6 NASB

Humble yourselves in the presence of the Lord, and He will exalt you. James 4:10 NASB.

To sum up, all of you be harmonious, sympathetic, brotherly, kindhearted, and humble in spirit;
1 Peter 3:8 NASB

You younger men, likewise, be subject to your elders; and all of you, clothe yourselves with humility toward one another, for GOD IS OPPOSED TO THE PROUD, BUT GIVES GRACE TO THE HUMBLE. Therefore, humble yourselves under the mighty hand of God, that He may exalt you at the

proper time, casting all your anxiety on Him,
because He cares for you.   1 Peter 5:5-7 NASB

Humility and mercy walk hand in hand. You cannot be merciful with an arrogant attitude. I have met some incredibly humble people in my life. Some of the humblest were in the most influential positions of church leadership you can imagine. When they spoke, they spoke with authority, when they talked to you they were gentle and kind, meek and humble. They could correct you and you would love them for the correction.

My mother-in-law would tell stories of her father's loving correction. I met Glenda, my wife, just after her Grandpa Bell passed away so I never got to meet him. But I got to know all four of his children. Betty, Wanda, Billy and Wayne. All four told similar stories of Grampa Bell's gentle spirit. I could tell you of others that I have met along the way, but it would go to bragging and that is not what I want. What I do want, is to remind you of someone you know who is humble before God and humanity. Not weak, but humble in their strength.

In most every church you will find one or two men, and a few women that are among the humblest people you will ever meet. They often don't get a lot of recognition because they are always promoting someone else, or quietly going about the role of serving in one manner or another. If you sing their praise it would embarrass them. They are deeply moved and embarrassed by accolades and praise. Walking among us are people who model the tool of humility effectively.

The funny thing about the humble is they don't think they are humble. My mom once said there was no ego in our family, because I had it all. Sadly, there was truth to that statement. Just as the humble are quick to say they are not, so is the person with a soaring ego quick to tell you they don't have one. I would encourage you to examine yourself carefully on this matter of humility. How you are perceived can go a long way in reaching someone who need Jesus as Savior. A humble spirit and heart will open doors to conversations that you can use to share Jesus.

False humility will ruin the opportunity. Carefully examine yourself and pray for a humble and meek spirit to become part of your life.

4. Justice

"You shall not distort justice; you shall not be partial, and you shall not take a bribe, for a bribe blinds the eyes of the wise and perverts the words of the righteous. "Justice, and only justice, you shall pursue, that you may live and possess the land which the LORD your God is giving you.
Deuteronomy 16:19-20 NASB

.

"You shall not pervert the justice due an alien or an orphan, nor take a widow's garment in pledge.
Deuteronomy 24:17 NASB

'Cursed is he who distorts the justice due an alien, orphan, and widow.' And all the people shall say, 'Amen.'
Deuteronomy 27:19 NASB

I have left justice to the end purposely. Notice if you will that as a requirement it is first. The distinction is "do justice." Moses recorded four times the same thought, and there are over 130 verses that contain the word Justice in the Bible.

In our world today as I write there are protests going on crying for justice and the end to racism. Racism is nothing if not justice averted. Justice is about treating every single person on the planet as equals. We are all created in the image of God. To imply or infer that another is "less" than we are is to deny the Love of God for His creation and puts us in danger of being cursed. If you have ever wondered why you have problems in your life, make sure you are walking in light of all the truths of God's Word. It will make a huge difference in your life.

I have a friend from college, Denny Curran. Rev. Curran pastors in Cold Springs, MN. He has planted more than 10 daughter churches. I was visiting him some 15 years ago and just down the street from their main church was a strip club, or at least there was a strip club in those days. He may have shut it down by down by now because of what happened.

The church decided to become proactive in praying for the women who worked at the club. Soon one of them stopped in at the church for help. She got saved. Before long she was bringing other girls to the church, and some were getting saved. The saved left the lifestyle of the club.

Here is the justice end of things. Some would refer to the girls as the "hookers," "strippers," and a few other choice words.

Let me ask you, do you wish to be known by what you were before you were a Christian? Or do you wish to be known as a Christian, saved by grace?

Doing justice in part means we stand up for the new Christian by declaring "all things have passed away and behold all things are new."

Doing justice means sticking up for those who are being taken advantage of in life.

Doing justice means fighting for the rights of the oppressed. Everyone deserves fair treatment. However, I deplore, hate, despise, and abhor evil. I will pray for you, with you and about you, but I will not let you continue in your evil without hearing the gospel.

Also, I will not let someone abuse you, denigrate you and hurt you because you have chosen a particular path. I can disagree with your choice all day long, and I will, but I will do justice on your behalf.

That is what Denny and the church decided to do, and as a result it was not just the women who started coming to church it was men who visited the club. That club lost a lot of patrons and employees because of the gospel and one man's decision to do justice.

The number one requirement from God's word in our tool box is "do justice." Will you stand up for people?

Conclusion:
Every tool you need to be a witness is in your Bible. We did not talk about the Roman Road, or the ABC's of salvation, or any other cleaver witnessing tool. I think of them as the nuts, bolts, nails and materials for building the project. Here is the truth. I cannot change a water pump on a car that is broken without a few tools. I can have a new water pump sitting right there, but without tools the car will still be broken. I have to employ the tools necessary to repair the problem

You have many tools in your "Spiritual Toolbox" for sharing the Gospel of Jesus Christ. I want to end this book with a challenge to begin using your spiritual tools to change a life.

ADDENDUM A

Psalm Thirty Day Reading Guide

	Chapter	Chapter	Chapter	Chapter	Chapter
Day 1	1	31	61	91	121
Day 2	2	32	62	92	122
Day 3	3	33	63	93	123
Day 4	4	34	64	94	124
Day 5	5	35	65	95	125
Day 6	6	36	66	96	126
Day 7	7	37	67	97	127
Day 8	8	38	68	98	128
Day 9	9	39	69	99	129
Day 10	10	40	70	100	130
Day 11	11	41	71	101	131
Day 12	12	42	72	102	132
Day 13	13	43	73	103	133
Day 14	14	44	74	104	134
Day 15	15	45	75	105	135
Day 16	16	46	76	106	136
Day 17	17	47	77	107	137
Day 18	18	48	78	108	138
Day 19	19	49	79	109	139
Day 20	20	50	80	110	140
Day 21	21	51	81	111	141
Day 22	22	52	82	112	142
Day 23	23	53	83	113	143
Day 24	24	54	84	114	144
Day 25	25	55	85	115	145
Day 26	26	56	86	116	146
Day 27	27	57	87	117	147
Day 28	28	58	88	118	148
Day 29	29	59	89	119	149
Day 30	30	60	90	120	150

ADDENDUM B

SCRIPTURE TO ENCOURAGE SEEKING GOD

And those who know Your name will put their trust in You, For You, O LORD, have not forsaken those who seek You.   Psalms 9:10 NASB

The LORD has looked down from heaven upon the sons of men to see if there are any who understand, who seek after God.   Psalms 14:2 NASB

The afflicted will eat and be satisfied; Those who seek Him will praise the LORD. Let your heart live forever!   Psalms 22:26 NASB

*One thing I have asked from the LORD, that I shall seek: That I may dwell in the house of the LORD all the days of my life, to behold the beauty of the LORD And to meditate in His temple.*Psalms 27:4 NASB

When You said, "Seek My face," my heart said to You, "Your face, O LORD, I shall seek."
                    Psalms 27:8 NASB

The young lions do lack and suffer hunger; But they who seek the LORD shall not be in want of any good thing.   Psalms 34:10 NASB

Let all who seek You rejoice and be glad in You; Let those who love Your salvation say continually, "The LORD be magnified!"   Psalms 40:16 NASB

God has looked down from heaven upon the sons of men to see if there is anyone who understands, who seeks after God.   Psalms 53:2 NASB

O God, You are my God; I shall seek You earnestly; My soul thirsts for You, my flesh yearns for You, in a dry and weary land where there is no water.
                    Psalms 63:1 NASB

The humble have seen it and are glad; You who seek God, let your heart revive.   Psalms 69:32 NASB

Glory in His holy name; Let the heart of those who seek the LORD be glad.   Psalms 105:3 NASB

How blessed are those who observe His testimonies, who seek Him with all their heart.
                    Psalms 119:2 NASB

"I love those who love me; And those who diligently seek me will find me.   Proverbs 8:17 NASB

Evil men do not understand justice, but those who seek the LORD understand all things.
                    Proverbs 28:5 NASB

BIBLIOGRAPHY

Chapter 1
    1. KJV King James Version of the Holy Bible

Chapter 2
    1. Random House Living Dictionary Project,
       Random House Webster's College Dictionary,
       New York, New York Random House, Inc. 1991.
       ISBN: 0-679-41420-7

    2. From a Mike Warnke 8 track tape circa 1975

    3. Dr. David R. Mains, Director, Mainstay
       Ministries, Chapel of the Air speaker
       mainstayministries.com

    4. The Five Love Languages, by Dr. Gary
       Chapman; Northfield Publishing, Chicago,
       Illinois. 1992, 1995, 2004.
       ISBN: 1-881273-15-6
       www.garychapman.org
       www.fivelovelanguages.com

    5. A wonderful resource for an electronic Bible is
       www.e-sword.net e-Sword is copyright Rick
       Myers and is free to use. There is information
       on donating to keep e-Sword free of charge.

Chapter 3
    1. Center for Disease Control website. United
       State Government
       https://www.cdc.gov/nchs/products/databriefs/db
       283.htm

2. Buechner, Frederick. Wishful Thinking: A Theological ABC's. New York, NY: Harper and Row, 1973. SBN: 06-061155-3

3. Matthew Henry 1662 – 1714; was a nonconformist minister and author, born in Wales but spent much of his life in England. He is best known for the six-volume biblical commentary Exposition of the Old and New Testaments. Source: Wikipedia

4. Barham, Cecil. The Dynamics of Forgiveness; Stopping the Hurts of Offenses Stopping You. North Charleston, South Carolina. CreateSpace Independent Publishing Platform. 1976, 2014 ISBN: 978-1482311624

Chapter 4
1. Jukes, Andrew. The Law of the Offerings: The Five Tabernacle Offerings and Their Spiritual Significance. Altenmünster, Germany. Jazzybee Verlag. 1847. ISBN: 13: 978-0825429767

2. Dorotheos of Gaz. Discourses and Sayings. Eric Wheeler OSB (Translator), Chrysogonus Waddell OCSO (Introduction). Collegeville, MN. Cistercian Publications. 1977 ISBN: 13: 978-0879079338

Chapter 5
1. Goggins, Gerard E. Half Wits. Ambassador Books. Melville, NY. 1988 ISBN: 10-1929039018

2. Roosevelt, Franklin D. When you reach the end of your rope, tie a knot in it and hang on. Source Brainy Quote,

https://www.brainyquote.com/quotes/franklin_d
_roosevelt_101840

Chapter 7

1. Narcissism, närsə‚sizəm, noun
   a. excessive interest in or admiration of oneself
      and one's physical appearance.
      Similar: vanity, self-love, self-admiration, self-
      adulation, self-absorption, self-obsession,
      conceit, self-conceit, self-centeredness, self-
      regard, egotism, egoism, egocentricity,
      egomania
      Opposite: modesty, diffidence

   b. selfishness, involving a sense of entitlement,
      a lack of empathy, and a need for
      admiration, as characterizing a personality
      type.

   c. self-centeredness arising from failure to
      distinguish the self from external objects,
      either in very young babies or as a feature of
      mental disorder.

      Oxford Dictionary U.S. Edition
      https://www.lexico.com/

2. ABHOR, verb [Latin abhorreo, of ab and horreo,
   to set up bristles, shiver or shake; to look
   terrible.]
   1. To hate extremely, or with contempt; to
   loathe, detest or abominate.
   2. To despise or neglect. Psalm 22:24. Amos 6:8.
   3. To cast off or reject. Psalm 89:38.

   Webster's Dictionary of the English Language
   1828 http//www.e-sword.com

3. See Matthew 5:39 and Luke 6:29

4. David's heart was wholly committed to God. For this reason, the phrase "a Man after God's own heart' has become popular. *For when Solomon was old, his wives turned his heart away after other gods; and his heart was not wholly devoted to the LORD his God, as the heart of David his father had been.* 1 Kings 11:4 NASB

Chapter 8

1. Newman, Jr, Barclay M. editor. A Concise Greek-English Dictionary of the New Testament. Stuttgart, West Germany: United Bible Societies. 1971

2. Vincent, D. D., Marvin R. Word Studies in the New Testament. Grand Rapids, Michigan Wm. B. Eerdmans 1887 reprinted 1975 ISBN: 0-8028-8083-5

3. Gaebelein, Frank E., General Editor. The Expositors Bible Commentary. Volume Ten Boice, James Montgomery Editor Galatians. Grand Rapids, Michigan. The Zondervan Corporation. 1976 ISBN: 0-310-36520-1

4. NIV. New International Version of the Holy Bible. International Bible Society and Zondervan Corporation publishers.

5. Nicoll M.A., LL. D, W. Robertson. The Expositors Greek Testament Volume Three Grand Rapids, Michigan. Wm. B. Eerdmans. 1983 ISBN 0-8028-2108-1

6. Jamieson, Robert; Fausset, Andrew Robert; Brown, David. Jameson-Fausset-Brown Bible Commentary. Grand Rapids, Michigan. Reprinted by The Zondervan Corporation. 1871

7. Harris M.A., Ralph W.; Horton Th.D., Stanley M.; Seaver J.D., Gayle Garity; Editors. The Complete Biblical Library, Galatians-Philemon. Springfield, Missouri. The Complete Biblical Library. 1995 ISBN 0-88243-368-7

8. Louw, Johannes P.; Nida, Eugene A; Editors. Greek-English Lexicon of the New Testament: Based on Semantic Domains, Second Edition. New York, New York. United Bible Societies 1988, 1999 ISBN: 0-8267-0343-7

9. Arichea, Daniel; Nida, Eugene. A Handbook on Paul's Letter to the Galatians. New York, New York. United Bible Societies. 1976. ISBN: 0-8267-0163-9

10. CEV. Contemporary English Version of the Bible. New York, New York. American Bible Society

11. ESV. The Holy Bible; English Standard Version Peabody, Massachusetts. Good News Publishers. 2001 ISBN: 978-1-59856-380-1

Chapter Ten
1. The Woman's Christian Temperance Union is an active international temperance organization that was among the first organizations of women devoted to social reform with a program that "linked the religious and the secular through concerted and far-reaching reform strategies based

on applied Christianity." The organization were instrumental in helping to bring about prohibition in the 1920's.
Founded on December 23, 1873, in Hillsboro, Ohio by Frances Willard and Annie Turner Wittenmyer.
http://www.wwctu.org/
Source: Wikipedia.

2. Toastmasters International is a non-profit educational organization that teaches public speaking and leadership skills through a worldwide network of clubs. Headquartered in Englewood, Colorado, the organization's membership exceeds 358,000 in more than 16,800 clubs in 143 countries. Founded October 22, 1924 by Ralph Smedley. Since its beginning Toastmasters International has helped people from diverse backgrounds become more confident speakers, communicators, and leaders.

Chapter Eleven

1. Perryman, Martin. The Helper, A devotional Study of the Person and Work of the Holy Spirit. Oklahoma City, Oklahoma 2019
   ISBN 9 781727 324907

2. Cohen, Leonard. Hallelujah. 1984

3. Shakespeare, William. The Merchant of Venice. Portia. Act 4 Scene 1
   https://shakespeare.folger.edu/shakespeares-works/the-merchant-of-venice/entire-play

Made in the USA
Monee, IL
20 August 2020